Developing
Speaking Skills

Developing Speaking Skills

Ceri James ◆ Mike Clarke ◆ Ann Woods

in association with

The views expressed in this publication are the authors' and do not necessarily represent those of CILT.

First published 1999

ISBN 1 902031 21 0

A catalogue record for this book is available from the British Library
Printed in Great Britain by Hazell Press

Published by the Centre for Information on Language Teaching and Research,
20 Bedfordbury, Covent Garden, London WC2N 4LB
Design: Charlie Tapper

CILT Publications are available from: Grantham Book Services, Isaac Newton Way, Alma Park Industrial Estate, Grantham, Lincs NG31 8SD. Tel: 01476 541 080.
Fax: 01476 541 061. Book trade representation (UK and Ireland): Broadcast Book Services, 24 De Montfort Road, London SW16 1LZ. Tel: 0181 677 5129.

Contents

Introduction

• Peter Boaks, Deputy Director CILT

The 1994 OHMCI publication *A Survey of Modern Foreign Languages in the National Curriculum in Wales* identified pupil performance in Attainment Target 2 (Speaking) as the weakest of the four language skills — *'Pupils' ability to speak the target language (TL) was unsatisfactory in just over half of the lessons seen, and good in only a small minority of schools. Few are able to use it spontaneously and fluently.'*

In 1995 CILT, the Welsh Office Education Department (WOED), OHMCI and the National Comenius Centre of Wales (NCCW) agreed to undertake a joint project to address the issues identified in the OHMCI document.

At the core of the project was an 'action research' programme involving 12 schools across Wales and supported by three regional Field Officers. Ceri James was a Field Officer and also managed the action research programme. The other Field Officers were Ann Woods and Mike Clarke. This phase covered the academic year 1996/97 and was linked to an HMI survey carried out in 20 schools during this period. Ten of those schools were participants in this project. We are particularly indebted to Steffan James HMI for his help and advice throughout.

Outcomes included:

- two national conferences in 1996 and 1997 — both held at Llandrindod Wells. The first set out the issues and intentions at the beginning of the action-research phase. The second reported back via presentations of case studies and of the OHMCI report Speaking Skills in Modern Foreign Languages;
- reports and evidence — a wealth of material including video — from teachers and pupils in the schools and from the Field Officers;
- this report from the Project Manager and Field Officers;
- input to the OHMCI survey on Speaking Skills in Modern Foreign Languages published in November 1997*;
- the dissemination of information on case studies, successful strategies and the lessons learned via progress bulletins, in-service training materials and meetings;
- the identification of a network of schools committed to exploring ways of improving their practice in order to increase pupil motivation and raise standards.

*Copies of the OHMCI report may be obtained from OHMCI, Phase 1, Government Buildings, Tŷ Glas Road, Llanishen, Cardiff CF4 5FQ

Main findings

The following summary list of issues, observations and conclusions draws on evidence from HMI, the Project Manager, the Field Officers and from the schools' own reports. The OHMCI survey was published in November 1997 and noted a positive impact made by the project in the ten participating schools which were included in the survey.

The project found that:

- participating in an official project was in itself a stimulating and motivating experience for both teachers and learners;
- the exchange of ideas between MFL teachers and Welsh L2 colleagues was a novel experience in some schools. This project was the catalyst for that. However it is clear that much remains to be done in this area;
- sharing teaching approaches and materials motivates teachers and raises their expectations of what pupils can achieve;
- the process of discussing specific focused strategies to encourage speaking made some departments very aware of the purely 'administrative' content of a normal departmental meeting;
- unless it is regularly assessed, Speaking is undervalued by pupils who are also unaware of their own standard and how they can progress. The HMI survey found increased motivation and better performance overall in schools which gave due importance to the assessment of speaking;
- a stimulating classroom environment and a real audience can have a marked impact on the motivation to speak;
- peer pressure helps — all must contribute. Year 10 boys responded well to drama techniques;
- some teachers were worried that over-emphasis on speaking activities was diverting them from their scheme of work — yet one at least attributed an observed improvement in creative writing to lively oral activities;
- increased confidence and fluency does not always imply improved accent or accuracy;
- even the most enthusiastic pupils rarely use the TL spontaneously amongst themselves. They respond to stimulus but few have developed the skill of working out what to say, either in response to the unpredictable or in situations requiring autonomy;
- activities need to engage the imagination and competitive spirit;
- pupils need short term rewards;
- teachers also need to learn to talk more to each other!

The School Projects

A brief description of the 12 school projects:

Cwm Gwendraeth	'Eurovillage' — construction and exploitation of a range of shops and other locations which enable pupils to practise their speaking skills in a more realistic setting. (French/German)
Pembroke	Developing a range of strategies including songs, raps and games to promote spontaneous use of the target language (TL) in Year 8. Improving pupil motivation. Introducing a merit scheme. (French/German/Spanish)
Amman Valley	Strategies to improve pupil confidence and fluency. Improving assessment techniques (including peer assessment). Developing pupil independence and spontaneity by gradually withdrawing written support. (French/German)
Mynyddbach	Developing self-confidence in speaking the target language through the use of songs, games, pairwork and group work, thus raising standards of oral work. (French/Welsh)
Darland	Using games, role-plays and drama techniques to encourage more extensive speaking amongst more able Year 10 pupils. Props used for authenticity, and pupil recordings made. A class video project. (French)
Ysgol Alun	Extending opportunities for use of TL in the classroom, (e.g. drama techniques, leading to Eisteddfod presentation) plus monitoring of progress (including peer and self-assessment). (French/Welsh)
Ysgol David Hughes	Improving pupils' ability to ask & respond to questions in Year 7, and 're-establishing' the TL as the language of the classroom in Year 9. Techniques included pupil recordings, and use of an aide-memoire or cue cards to encourage longer exchanges. (French/German)
Croesyceiliog	Study of why success in Year 7 and 8 does not always carry on to KS4 (need to 're-acquire' strategies; reasons for 'plateau'). (French/German)
Glan Ely	Enhancement of pronunciation, accuracy & fluency by increasing use of games, pair/group work and listening exercises. Introduction of merit scheme. (French)
Abersychan	Increasing spontaneity through pair/group work, listening activities and introducing an element of grammar. (French/German)
Lewis Girls	Development of learner strategies; differentiation; assessment and recording. Cross-fertilisation of ideas and strategies across departments. (French/Welsh/Italian/Japanese)
Maelor School	Encouraging use of TL by helping pupils internalise essential structures and patterns. Drama techniques to improve motivation and increase pupil confidence. (French/Welsh)

The lessons

The HMI survey concludes that 'the CILT/NCCW project has had a very beneficial effect in raising awareness and improving provision and practice in the 12 schools involved'. The survey also has a list of main recommendations for raising standards further. Issues raised by the schools and the Field Officers in the final project reports reinforce those recommendations.

The nature of the project and the way in which it was conceived and run have been fully vindicated by the reactions of the participants. To quote from the Project Bulletin of March 1997: 'All three Field Officers would like to take this opportunity to congratulate teachers and pupils on the effort and imagination which they have put into the Speaking Skills Project. The school visits have been an enjoyable and heartening experience for all concerned'.

This judgement of the Field Officers is reciprocated by the schools. For example, one states: 'Involvement in the project also allowed two younger teachers (Welsh, French/Italian) to attend the national conference which, given INSET budget constraints, they might not otherwise have been able to do. This, together with their visit to another school and meetings for teachers from other schools involved in the project, was valuable professional development for them. Their insights have been shared with the rest of the school team.'

Another enthuses: 'A stimulating project which has enriched us all.'

Yet another observes that 'since embarking on the project the level of interaction between staff has increased considerably; further, it has been interaction with a specific purpose and has therefore been more focused. This sharing has generated a feast of ideas and strategies, and proved that we are more imaginative and inventive than we thought we were!'

Several schools asked the pupils themselves to evaluate the project as it proceeded. One reports: 'The pupils' self-assessment confirms my feelings. The project has enabled me to establish a better relationship with the group, sharing their sense of achievement and touched by the warmth and enthusiasm of their response. Merci Comenius.'

Perhaps the clearest message from the project is that motivation matters. This is as true for teachers as it is for pupils.

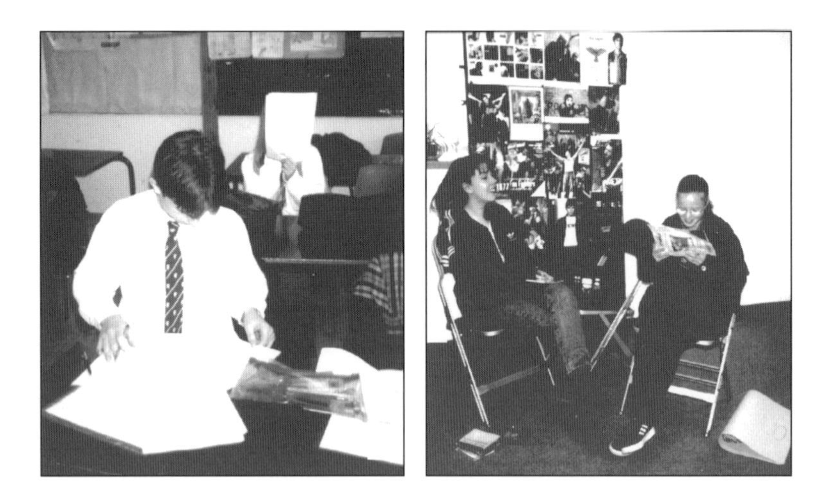

Chapter One

Getting things into perspective

• Ann Woods

> A small pig approaches a wild owl in tears. She explains to the owl that she needs to learn to fly so that she will be able to hunt for food. 'That's easy', says the owl, 'just go away and grow wings'. So the small pig goes away and struggles to grow wings. When this doesn't work, she goes back to complain that it's not as easy as the owl made out. 'Don't blame me', comes back the answer. 'Owls are only responsible for policy and strategy. Implementation is up to the pig'.

When I first came out of the classroom to work as an adviser, there were two things which took me a long time to get used to. The first was that, overnight, I had become an owl. No more snuffling around the 'well, it might be . . .' or ' I really haven't a clue'; wisdom was required immediately and, if not wisdom, then the appearance of certainty and infallibility would do. It can be very easy for owls to come to think that they really know more than pigs. But as you fly over the territory and perch in so many different classrooms, the second factor strikes you — that you have read as much as you have time for, you have been to conferences and Insets, you have developed all kinds of strategies in your own department, your knowledge is partial, individual. The question that you quickly begin to ask is 'why didn't I think of that', 'why didn't I do that', or, more worryingly 'Oh no, I used to do that all the time, isn't it awful'. I think that has also been the experience of many schools in the Project. Teaching can be a very lonely business; despite the growth of departmental team-work, there is still a sense in which one is in one's own shop, behind the closed door. One of the most positive spin-offs of the Project has been the development of a way of working which has brought together teachers within one department, or teachers in MFL and Welsh second language departments, schools in local clusters and across Wales, not only to work on their own classes but to observe and discuss practice in a much wider context than is usually the case. Everyone should get the opportunity to spread their wings and fly about a bit.

In my experience, the vast majority of teachers want to get better at what they do. But it easy to get dispirited, particularly in view of the increasing and never ending demands which are made on teachers, many of whom rightly say that they could not work any harder. But again, the experience of the Project schools would suggest that improvements can be brought about, not by working harder but by developing a clear focus on specifically identified aspects of teaching and learning. It is interesting that many of the schools chose similar aspects for their work. Different teachers, different schools, different environments came up with remarkably similar problems and strategies to deal with them. But identifying the problems and strategies is only the first step. Target setting is one of the new buzz words among the owls. It is not always possible to set measurable targets in speaking — we are often looking for an increase in self-confidence and a willingness to 'have a go'. But there are aspects of oral production which lead to better performance — length of utterance, use of a range of vocabulary, structures and tenses, ranging across different topics etc which are more objectively measurable. The process of planning and producing reflection grids, although sometimes felt to be extra paperwork, was felt by schools to be useful. Schools could not just bathe in the warm glow which can sometimes come from feeling that 'we're trying to make it better, therefore it must be actually getting better', but had to comment and to set new aims or targets for the next session. As one school said: 'It kept us on the straight and narrow'.

Target setting, reflection and evaluation are also major components of any assessment process. Those schools which had identified improved assessment of oral skills as a Project aim found this to have been an unexpectedly productive element of their work. Not only have they devised ways of assessing oral work more regularly and effectively, but they have found that the act of defining more clearly in their own minds precisely what the characteristics of good speaking are (often using the National Curriculum level descriptors as a useful tool rather than a bothersome piece of paperwork) has sharpened up their own ability to move pupils onward more consistently. Those schools which have shared these criteria with the pupils themselves have reported an increase in pupils' willingness and ability to at least try to meet the criteria.

Assessment can be used to motivate pupils. And what else? The atmosphere of lessons is, of course, crucial. Clearly the teachers involved in the Project had chosen to take part, so it is not surprising that the activities in classes were demanding. But despite the increased demands, the atmosphere was relaxed and friendly, pupils had to feel able to take more risks, to make mistakes without the fear of mockery or disapproval. Praise and reward were part of much practice, although I do fear for the teeth of the nation's children if too many sweets are handed out in MFL lessons! The competitive element was also a feature in many classrooms. The use of drama — dressing up, acting out, developing real scenarios has also been a success, particularly with boys. Perhaps these activities take the edge off the fear of speaking, attention is concentrated on the task, not the unnatural act of speaking in a foreign language to your mates on a wet Thursday in Wales. Perhaps such activities bring us nearer to why we speak in the first place — we have something we want to say and are less worried about getting the words in the right order than in saying our piece.

This reminder of how we first begin to speak lead me on to what my family calls 'The Tommy test'. My grandson, when he was learning to speak, did not go through the 'why' phase. His question was always 'what for is this?' Not always an easy question to answer — grass, sea, having to go to bed every night — what for is it? It is a question I often ask myself when sitting in classrooms. What for is this task? How does it move these children forward? What can they do that they couldn't before? What can they do at the end of the lesson that they couldn't do when they came in? There is so much good material in the new course books which most teachers are using that there is a tendency to do it all, to work one's way through it. Some Project schools expressed worry that, in increasing the time spent on speaking, they were getting behind with the scheme of work, which, in most schools means the course book. Teachers are conscientious and do not want to miss anything out 'in case it comes up later on'. This is particularly clear when assessment, usually testing, is closely linked to the particular way in which language is presented in the course. But course books bring their own problems. One often sees activities which are too hard for the least able, or which do not challenge the more able. The problem becomes more acute as we move up into Years 9, 10 and 11. Pupils are sometimes involved in low level tasks, often around Level 2 and 3, even in Years 9 and 10. The past tense sometimes disappears altogether for months at a time. Progression in the middle stages of the courses is a real problem. Project schools were often all too aware of what was happening, and approached it in different ways. One dropped the course book altogether for oral work and concentrated on creative, imaginative activities. The danger they encountered was that they began to run out of time to prepare pupils for the specific demands of the GCSE examination. But the spin-off in enhanced performance and motivation is such that they have decided to compromise and adapt the GCSE scheme of work to include imaginative work on existing GCSE topics. Another very experienced Head of Faculty has been convinced for some time that, in her own words, course books limit pupils' language. In doing too much you can, paradoxically, end up doing too little. The vast amount of language available in listening tape scripts, for example, is reduced to background verbiage; pupils are rarely asked to do more than pick out information, when material could in fact be used to stimulate, extend and reinforce pupils' language skills at all levels.

It may seem perverse to complain that we suffer from such interesting course books. They present language in interesting ways, pupils are carefully led through a process of acquisition, practice, consolidation and use. But for many pupils, the foreign language is what is in the book, it is predictable, can be learned by heart and reproduced in manageable chunks. You and I know that language is not like that. And MFL teachers are, of course, not alone with the problem. A colleague of mine who works with science teachers and is a cricket fanatic uses a cricketing analogy to describe the same situation: teachers work tremendously hard to set up the nets, to get the children to go there, to give them plenty of practice. Pupils learn a great deal and eventually more or less master all the shots they are likely to meet. But very few of them ever come out of the nets and play the game for real. It is to the enormous credit of MFL teachers that they recognise that, although enormous effort has gone into getting pupils to play a wider variety of strokes than ever before, there is still some way to go before the majority of pupils are playing the real game.

A number of the Project schools began with a concern that weaknesses in speaking became clearer as pupils moved through the national curriculum. Teachers in my own cluster, in discussion after the first stimulating Project conference in Autumn 1996, were enthused by the ideas presented for improving speaking in Year 7, but felt that Year 7 is not the problem, the problem is in Years 9 and 10. I have touched on my own worries about the slowness of progression in many schemes of work. The experience gained with Year 9 and Key Stage 4 pupils, described in the report, has proved very valuable. But there is no doubt that schools have shown that much more can be expected of all pupils, including Year 7. From very early on, many pupils can speak at length, they can ask as well as answer questions, they can speak from memory or from visual or one word prompts rather than scripts; once they understand how to transfer language learned in one topic into a new situation, they respond to the challenge.

Challenge is another of our current buzz words. It seems that teachers' work is never done. You have gone through CSE, GCSE, TVEI, mixed ability, SEN, national curriculum, and you have made them all work but still it's not quite good enough, you don't challenge them sufficiently. Perhaps the same contention would be more acceptable if expressed differently: in your classroom, who is working harder, the teacher or the pupil? If the answer is the teacher, perhaps a little redressing of the balance might be no bad thing. I said earlier that, in my experience, teachers want to get better at what they do. A teacher in one of the schools said: 'We didn't want a project to stick up on the wall, glossy pictures and a nice bit of word processed text, to look good on open days or for inspection. It was such a change to be involved in something we had chosen ourselves, which we thought was important, and which we thought could really make a difference'.

There is always the worry, at the end of a project, that the momentum will go, the work will be forgotten, and real life will take over. I do hope that this time it will be different. One of the most productive elements of the Project has been the way that different strands of the MFL family have worked together. CILT has been not a faceless organisation in far off London, but a real stimulus to action; the Comenius centres have provided us with resources and a new point of contact for support; the field officers have been able to link their work in inspection, Inset, and the WJEC to the experience emerging from the Project; HMI have visited the schools and produced an excellent report on speaking which draws partly on observations made there; and as ever, the teachers and pupils in the schools involved have done all the hard work, which subsequent chapters of this book analyse in detail. It doesn't actually make any difference if you are an owl, a pig or a beast of your own choosing, what matters is that we care enough to 'have a go' to try and make a difference.

Chapter Two

Characteristics of pupil performance in the project schools

•Ceri James

This chapter focuses on some of the pupil activities which took place in the 12 project schools during the school year, and will highlight the successes and failures which were reported by the teachers involved.

In the reports from individual schools, teachers described the main characteristics of pupil performance in speaking, and it soon became clear that a number of themes and preoccupations were common to them all. These included:

- Increasing the complexity of language — how do we encourage pupils to make the longer utterance and how do we enable them to speak at length?
- Increased confidence, creativity and enjoyment can lead to an improved performance in speaking. How do we extend this improvement to other areas (e.g. writing)?
- Fluency versus Accuracy. How do we improve accuracy without discouraging the pupils and undermining their confidence/fluency?
- What are the reasons for the perceived levelling-off (or plateau) of achievement in Year 9? What can be done to improve the situation?

These are important questions, and although the project schools found no miracle cures or 'quick fixes', the activities which they developed and the teachers' reflections on how they worked do provide some interesting pointers for fellow professionals.

Development of the target language

In recent years teachers have made sterling efforts to implement the National Curriculum Programmes of Study for MFL, and have radically increased the use of the target language as the normal means of communication in the classroom. Great strides have been made, but several of the project schools perceived that these strides become more faltering as the pupils enter Year 9.

At this stage the target language tends to be used less frequently by both teacher and pupils, and the range of language available to the pupils does not expand sufficiently to meet their needs. With the pressures of GCSE work in Years 10 and 11, there is a danger than this trend can continue into Key Stage 4, thus bringing about the unfortunate situation whereby the pupils may make less active use of the target language at 16 years of age than they did at the age of 11.

A number of schools decided to take active steps to remedy this situation, and made a concerted effort to re-establish the target language as the language of the classroom in Year 9.

For example: 'We began by deciding the types of phrases/vocabulary (the language they would need to know in class) that Year 9 should be able to cope with, which would differentiate them from Year 7. We began by revising phrases learnt earlier and looked at expanding them. We began with the following areas:

- Command instructions
  - — What the teacher may say to the pupils and what pupils may say to each other
- Homework routines
  - — Why they have/have not done homework
  - — Their reactions to the homework
- Question forms
  - — What pupils ask each other and the teacher
- Pupils generally chatting to each other about non-subject specific interests
  - — What they did last night
  - — General chit-chat
- Reasons — excuses for absence
  - — Elaborating on excuse/reasons for not doing something or wanting to do something
  - — Being late — no homework
- Explanation of language/grammar points
  - — Asking for clarification
  - — Saying that you have understood/not understood something

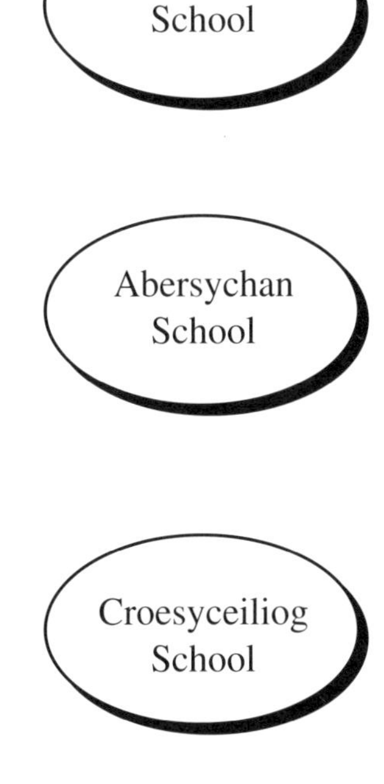

Teachers at *Alun School, Mold* found that pupils responded well when they were given the opportunity to personalise such language for their own use, and 5-10 minutes of each lesson were devoted to practising the expanded range of phrases. A small beanbag or ball was used to focus the mind — the teacher would throw it to a pupil whilst asking a question, and the pupil would answer whilst sending the ball back to the teacher. Not a new idea, but simple, effective and fun.

The pupils also developed mobiles with key words and phrases in the target language on one side and in the mother tongue on the other. Such visual support was also successful in *Abersychan School*, where headings such as 'Confused?', 'Need Help?', 'Requests' and 'Equipment' helped pupils to identify 'help vocabulary' and allowed them to continue with an activity which might otherwise have broken down. It was found to be less confusing for pupils if all the help vocabulary for French was displayed on one side of the classroom, and that for German was put on the opposite side. Other schools put backing paper of different colours behind the displays in order to achieve the same goal. Obviously all such wall displays need to be clearly laid out and legible from all parts of the classroom.

At *Croesyceiliog School*, *Cwmbrân*, the department systematically revised its scheme of work in order to ensure that classroom use of the target language was developing appropriately, giving opportunities to revise language which had already been taught, whilst expanding the range of words and phrases at the pupils' disposal. All pupils were expected to present excuses for lateness/non-submission of homework in the target language, and all displayed confidence and a willingness to speak in the classroom.

One of the major plus points of the project for the staff was that it re-focused their minds on teaching methods and departmental policy. It is no doubt true in a majority of schools that too much time is spent in department meetings discussing purely 'administrative' matters such as ordering books and equipment, school reports, arrangements for the exchange visit, etc, etc! Heads of Department may have to make an effort to ensure that the effective teaching of languages and methodology remain important agenda items!

A.	B.
Wie heißt ..... *auf deutsch*?	Wie heißt ..... *auf deutsch*?
Wie schreibt man das?	Wie schreibt man das?
Was bedeutet .....?	Was bedeutet .....?

A.		B.	
clock?	....	cheap?	....
puzzle?	....	newspaper?	....
cross (x)?	....	tick?	....
Russia?	....	I don't know?	....
It's your go!	....	Be quite!	....
Radfahren?	....	*Kopfhörer?*	....
dort drüben?	....	*vielleicht*	....
Bein?	....	*Zeit?*	....
Halskette?	....	*Geld?*	....
manchmal?	....	*spät?*	....

A.	B.
der Kopfhörer — Walkman	*Russland* — Russia
Sei ruhig! — be quiet	*das Kreuz* — cross (x)
der Haken — tick (✓	*die Uhr* — clock
vielleicht — perhaps	*manchmal* — sometimes
die Zeitung — newspaper	*die Halskette* — necklace
das Geld — money	*dort drüben* — over there
ich weiß nicht — I don't know	*das Rätsel* — puzzle
billig — cheap	*Radfahren* — cycling
spät — late	*Jetzt bist du dran!* — it's your turn!
die Zeit — time	*das Bein* — leg

Pupil worksheet — Croesyceiliog

Increasing complexity of language

A recent OHMCI survey into speaking skills in MFL found that in the lessons in which standards were good or very good, pupils' speaking was characterised by:

- use of complex sentences;
- ability to adapt in a new context language which had previously been learnt in another;
- ability to adapt and re-use the language of a question in formulating an answer.

Amman Valley Comprehensive School

Departmental Discussion Point
What is your policy regarding the development/ extension of target language use in years 9-11?

At *Amman Valley Comprehensive School* teachers concentrated on building up the complexity and length of pupil utterances, and found that the key to achieving this lay in the provision and progressive withdrawal of support:

'We have identified two distinct types of support sheet: those which give support in terms of the structures needed to complete the task and those which give a reminder of the sort of content which has been learnt. The former need to be withdrawn gradually so that real independence can be achieved by the pupil. The latter can consist of pictures or headings and can be kept before the pupil until (s)he decides that (s)he has exhausted its possibilities and wishes to speak more independently/ spontaneously/ ambitiously.'

The teachers made good use of OHP pictures and flashcards in this preparatory/ drilling phase, which served as a useful 'aide-memoire' until the language had been internalised. The other major advantage of visual prompts is that they do not interfere with pronunciation, which can be an unfortunate by-product of over-reliance on written prompts, especially in French.

The pupils' final, prompt-free utterings would sometimes be captured on video, which allowed them to assess their own performance. They realised that they were successfully engaging in 'spontaneous' discussions, and were able to cope with changes of direction and topic. They had to draw on the language they had learnt and re-cycle it in a different context. They saw the value of 'communication repair strategies' which allowed them to dig themselves out of conversational holes.

The transcript below shows the excellent results which were achieved by able Year 9 pupils; what it cannot convey is their confidence, fluency, enjoyment and sense of fun!

Transcript of video recording - Amman Valley School
(occasional errors also transcribed)

Activity: unscripted conversation
Pupils: Year 9 girls Meleri and Lowri
Written support : none

L: Qu'est-ce que tu seras dans 20 ans?
M: Moi, dans 20 ans je serai médecin dans un grand hôpital à Paris . J'aime les sciences.
L: Je serai avocate . . . et d'abord je travaillerai à Londres et puis j'habiterai à Zimbabwe parce que je serai riche — je ne travaillerai pas.
M: Euh! Moi, je déteste l'Afrique! L'année dernier je suis allée à Afrique du Sud et les hommes est racistes!
L: Non!

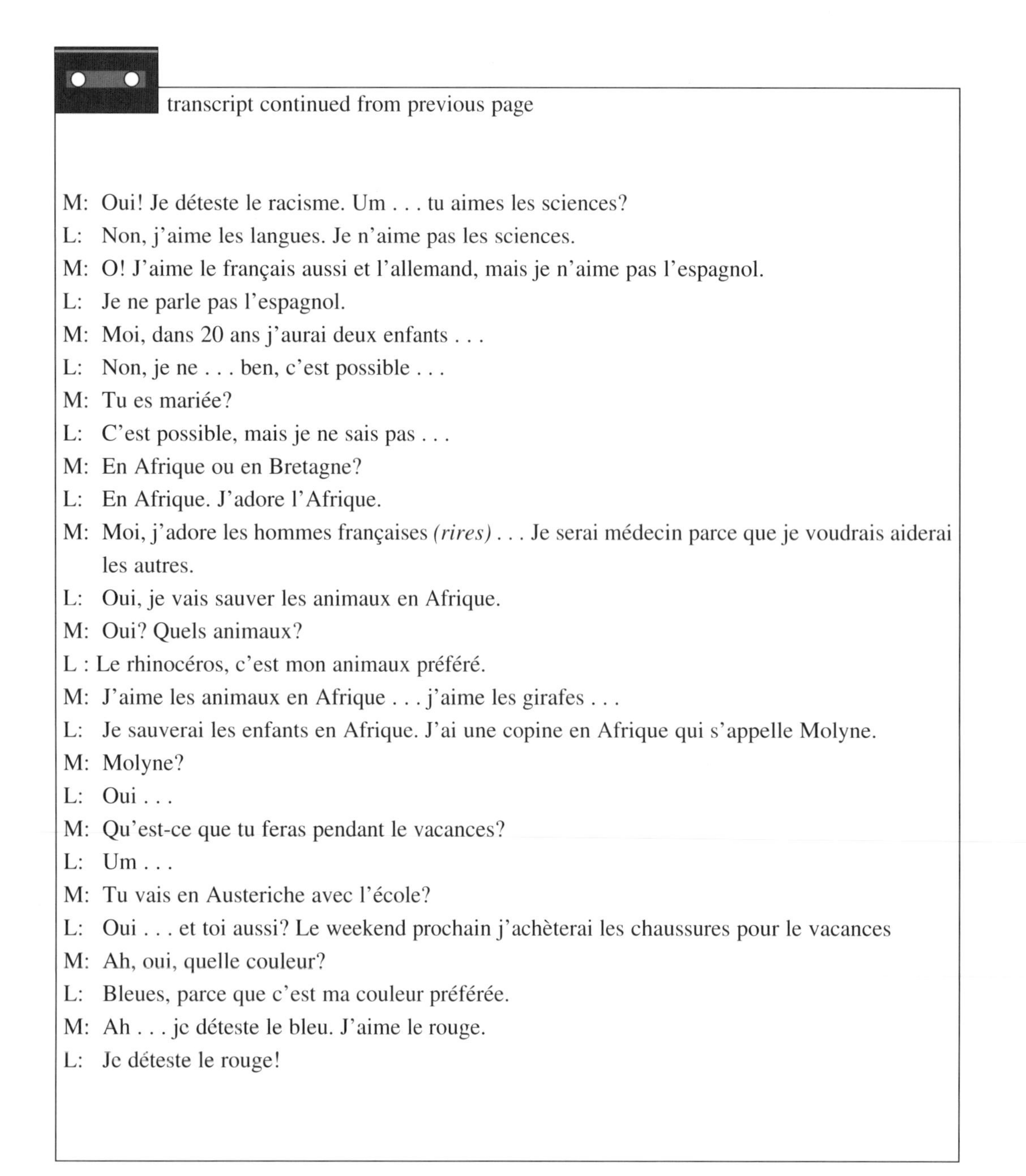
transcript continued from previous page

M: Oui! Je déteste le racisme. Um . . . tu aimes les sciences?
L: Non, j'aime les langues. Je n'aime pas les sciences.
M: O! J'aime le français aussi et l'allemand, mais je n'aime pas l'espagnol.
L: Je ne parle pas l'espagnol.
M: Moi, dans 20 ans j'aurai deux enfants . . .
L: Non, je ne . . . ben, c'est possible . . .
M: Tu es mariée?
L: C'est possible, mais je ne sais pas . . .
M: En Afrique ou en Bretagne?
L: En Afrique. J'adore l'Afrique.
M: Moi, j'adore les hommes françaises *(rires)* . . . Je serai médecin parce que je voudrais aiderai les autres.
L: Oui, je vais sauver les animaux en Afrique.
M: Oui? Quels animaux?
L : Le rhinocéros, c'est mon animaux préféré.
M: J'aime les animaux en Afrique . . . j'aime les girafes . . .
L: Je sauverai les enfants en Afrique. J'ai une copine en Afrique qui s'appelle Molyne.
M: Molyne?
L: Oui . . .
M: Qu'est-ce que tu feras pendant le vacances?
L: Um . . .
M: Tu vais en Austeriche avec l'école?
L: Oui . . . et toi aussi? Le weekend prochain j'achèterai les chaussures pour le vacances
M: Ah, oui, quelle couleur?
L: Bleues, parce que c'est ma couleur préférée.
M: Ah . . . je déteste le bleu. J'aime le rouge.
L: Je déteste le rouge!

The above extract shows how structured activities can lead on to more open-ended and creative work.

The same process was observed in *Ysgol y Gwendaeth's* 'Eurovillage', where the realistic village setting seemed to inspire pupils to produce more creative and imaginative conversations. However the 'Eurovillage' alone could not bring about the desired complexity of language — careful planning was also required.

A Year 8 class used the café and the market stalls to enhance work on the themes of 'shopping' and 'food'. During the first term, the work developed as follows:

Departmental Discussion Point
What sort of preparatory work do you think preceded the conversation transcribed above? How did the pupils keep up the momentum of their discussion?

Term 1

1) Role-play in cafe/market — pupils have prompt cards, tasks to perform.

2) More open-ended tasks.

3) Creation of own situations.

In Term 2, the following elements were added:

Term 2

1) Pupils given questions to ask to elicit information.

2) Pupils given short prompts.

3) Pupils given a subject, but create their own questions.

4) Pupils select a topic, and interview an 'inhabitant' of the 'Eurovillage'.

In Terms 2-3, problem-solving activities were introduced which allowed pupils to cope with unexpected events, for example a theft/robbery/kidnap/murder. From answering closed questions alone, pupils were encouraged to answer more open questions.

The same settings were used with different year groups, with appropriate changes to the nature and complexity of the tasks. The staff were constantly attempting to 'stretch' their pupils, who responded well to these high expectations. Here is how the school made good use of the café setting with different year groups:

Pages taken from the Gwendraeth report

Example of the use of 1 unit : The Cafe

Year 7: Simple transactional language eg "A coffee and a croissant please".

Gathering simple information eg where the shopkeepers live.

Authentic setting for French breakfasts/mini meals.

Year 8: More complex transactional language - "Do you have ...... please/thank you". "Well can I have ....."

More detailed information gathering.

Activity eg robbery in which pupils describe who stole the pizza!

Year 9: Full conversation ordering food in a cafe - ordering a full meal.

Finding out more complex information - eg how the shopkeeper is related to other people in the "village".

Further activities - to fit in with scheme of work.

Years 10/11 GCSE role play practice - reserving a table, situation of the table, ordering a meal, paying the bill, asking for clarification of the menu etc.

Finding out information from the "inhabitants" eg what there is to do in and around the village.

Problem solving activities eg reacting to a "kidnapping" outside the cafe etc.

Years 12/13 Will act as waiters/waitresses for younger pupils who will have to find out attitudes/ opinions of cafe personnel to environmental issues or political issues. They will have to compare and contrast the ideas of two of the "villagers". More advanced students will have to negotiate to sell a product eg a new drinks machine to the cafe owner.

Pupils will create their own situations at an elementary, intermediate or advanced level. With easy access the lenght of the visit will be tailored to pupil requirement.

Other Regulaar Uses

The "Eurovillage" will provide an ideal setting:

- for the language assistants to conduct their withdrawal lessons.
- for the foreign language clubs (French, German, Swedish) meet.
- to practise for the "Festival of Languages" in which Gwendraeth always takes part.
- for French breakfasts/mini-meals

Staffing:

a The classteacher and small groups.
b The classteacher and assistant and trainess and/or Yr 12/13 "A" level pupils with larger groups.
c The foreign languages assistants and small groups.
d The trainee teachers and small groups.

Special Events:

It is hoped that we shall be able to arrange special foreign language events in the "Eurovillage", eg a French day, a German day, a European day - This will involve foreign nationals living in the local community in "manning the village" or if possible, one day will be set aside for the trainee teachers from Hendrefoilan to run the village.

We shall certainly capitalize on the exchange visits and use the French/German pupils and staff when they come over to Wales to staff the "village" with native speakers.

Assessment:

Assessment will take various forms:

1 As a pupil carries out a task the teacher etc notes details of the task and a mark is given for how well the task has been carried out.
2 Worksheets will be completed and other written assignments set.
3 Interviews/tasks will be recorded on either cassette or video for analysis in the classroom.

Future Uses:

The "Eurovillage" will hopefully be used by language learners in the local community and other schools. If the three full-time MFL staff were able to have two of their non-contact periods together on the same afternoon once per fortnight this would ensure that three teachers and assistants and trainees would be available to run "the village" for use by others.

We also hope that one unit per year will change thus ensuring continuous renewal.

Such a facility for foreign language learning will enrich the cultural and linguistic experiences of pupils of all ages and abilties, regardless of how long they have been learning a foreign language all the time. It must be associated with this and be completely free of any English or Welsh which pupils see and hear around them everyday. Indeed they only have to walk five minutes up the road to be in an authentic village street. The "Eurovillage" will provide a French/German street which is as authentic as possible and which provides a stimulating, supporting environment for using their foreign languages(s).

Gwendraeth School

Obviously the physical resource of a 'Eurovillage' cannot be reproduced in every school, but there are a number of lessons which can be learnt from the Gwendraeth experience :

- pupils respond well to realistic activities (settings, props, clothing, etc.);
- more open-ended activities spark pupils' imagination and can extend their language;
- the same scenario/topic can be revisited with an increased level of challenge/ unpredictability for pupils, and with a different focus;
- many pupils are capable of much more than GCSE-type role-play activities, and benefit from being stretched further.

Drama Techniques

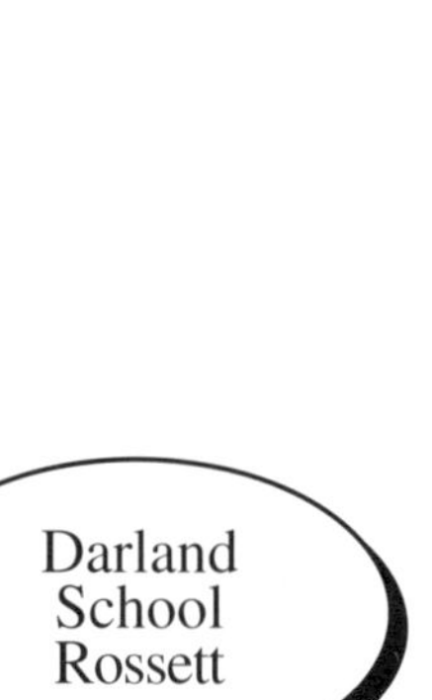

Darland School Rossett

Other project schools found that drama techniques could usefully be employed to extend pupils' speaking skills in Key Stage 4. In *Darland School, Rossett* pupils produced an impressive *télémagazine* on video, including interviews about smoking and ecological issues, pop music reviews, a fashion show and an item featuring a French version of the Spice Girls. The teacher in charge describes the preparatory process:

'Phase 1 was confidence building and broadening the vocabulary base of the pupils involved via games, role-plays and interviews. These were extended in the next phase into more complex situations and characterisation.

The project succeeded best when it was closely linked with topics on-going in the classroom as part of the Scheme of Work and related to the coursebook. The latter provided vocabulary support and grammatical structures on which pupils could base their preparatory work. The less successful attempts came early on when situations were plucked from thin air and were superimposed on existing classroom and lesson content.'

The preparations for filming involved a great deal of individual, pair and group work on scripting of items, which had a positive effect on pupils' written work. On the following page is an example of a script.

The Head of Department's initial fears about the project's effect on progression through the GCSE course had been banished by the end of the school year:

'Pupils have better reading skills than their counterparts in recent years and their writing tasks have been enhanced by practice within the project — i.e. they can write accurately and with more extended description and opinion.'

Mynyddbach School Swansea

Mynyddbach School, Swansea also achieved considerable success with younger pupils in French and Welsh 2nd Language, using songs, raps, sketches and extended role plays to boost confidence and improve fluency and pronunciation. Again, support was gradually withdrawn so that pupils could eventually reproduce lengthy pieces of language from memory. Motivation was increased by the pupils' awareness that they were preparing to perform in front of an audience (firstly their class-mates, followed by the school and national 'Eisteddfodau').

From an initial dependency on scripts, pupils gradually became 'hungry' for more language which allowed them to become involved in more creative and imaginative work. The pupils themselves were now leading the way towards longer utterances.

Secrets
by Helen Tattersall and Cheryl Warburton

Characters- Veronique (Grandmother)- Catherine Bibby
David (Father)- Steven Witham
Annie (Mother)- Nicky Hylands
Marie (Daughter)- Helen Tattersall
Pierre (Son)- Chris Jones
Martine (Daughter)- Emma Arkley
Christine - Delyth Hughes
Isabelle - Helena McGivern
Sophie - Clair Saunders
Natacha - Cheryl Warburton.

SCENE ONE

(Annie, David, and Veronique in the sitting room.)

Veronique Où sont les enfants?

David Je sais pas. (shrugs shoulders) Marie, Pierre, Martine!

(enter Pierre)

Pierre Oui papa?

David Où sont tes soeurs?

Pierre Marie est sortie avec Patrik, et Martine est au téléphone. Ça m'énerve parce que elle passe sa vie au téléphone et alors moi je ne peux jamais téléphoner.

Annie Ça m'énerve moi aussi, mais ne mentionne pas ça.

(enter Martine)

Martine Changez la chaine, je préfére les dessins animes. Les actualites sont enneyeuses.

Pierre Non, tu as trop egoïste......

page 1

Annie Mes enfants, ne disputez pas.

(they watch some TV)

(enter Marie, she sits down and looks uncomfortable)

Annie Bonjour Marie.

Marie Salut.

Annie Qu'est-ce qu'il y a?

Marie Rien.

Annie Vraiment?

Marie Non, Patrik m'a proposé le mariage.

(All gasp)

David Et.......

Marie Et j'ai dit oui.

Annie Oh! Marie.

Marie Maman j'adore Patrik.

David Tu as trop jeune.

Marie Papa, j'ai dix-huit ans!

(she storms out, crying)

SCENE TWO

(Marie, Christine, Isabelle, Sophie and Natacha in Marie's bedroom)

(Marie is crying her friends are comforting her.)

Christine N'inquietez-toi pas!

page 2

Isabelle Calme-toi!

Natacha Ils vont accepter ça, bien sûr.

Sophie Au moins , tu n'es pas adopte, comme moi!

Isabelle Et ton petit ami ne t'a pas quitté avec ton père!

Marie Quoi! Tu rigoles!

Isabelle C'est vrai.

(Marie, Sophie, Isabelle and Christine all cry)

Natacha Tais-toi! Je suis enceinte!

(All cry and comfort each other)

(outside the door Martine stands listening)

Martine Très interessant!

(laughs manically)

END

page 3

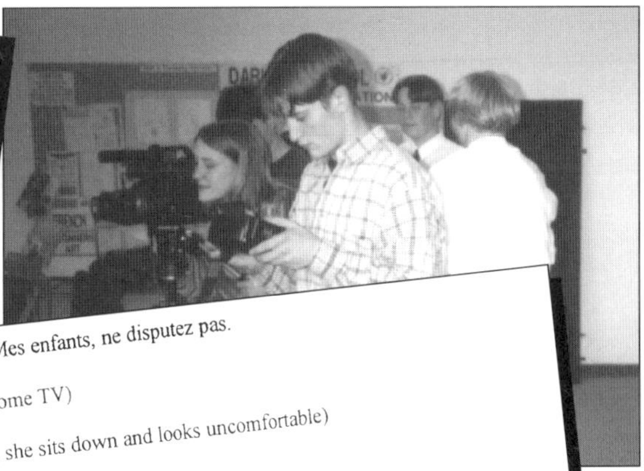

Darland School.

Recycling language

A number of schools were aware that learners were sometimes allowed to be too passive in class. Listening comprehension activities are of course useful for assessment purposes, but all too often the language encountered is not actively used or 'recycled' by pupils. *Alun School, Mold* decided to address this problem directly:

'We made a concerted effort to exploit the use of tape scripts by producing them for the pupils as:

- *gap-fill exercises;*
- *to put into correct order according to the tape;*
- *to use as a model for their own speaking or writing;*
- *to use as extension material for more able students.'*

The school's ITT student produced a booklet which developed the use of tape scripts, and the pupils were encouraged to use the personal expressions and extended vocabulary found in it.

'Listening activities are readily differentiated by what we ask pupils to do. Much of the language is missed by the majority of pupils. We encouraged pupils to listen for the more unusual phrases and re-use them later in phrases of their own.'

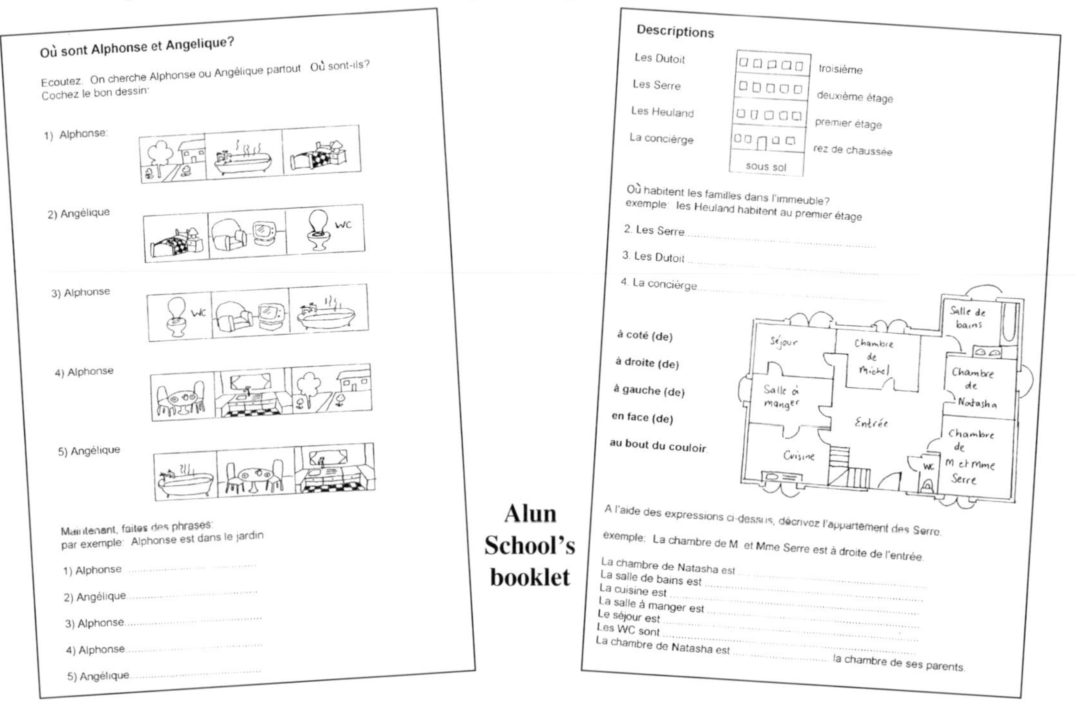

Où sont Alphonse et Angelique?

Ecoutez. On cherche Alphonse ou Angélique partout. Où sont-ils? Cochez le bon dessin:

1) Alphonse:

2) Angélique

3) Alphonse

4) Alphonse

5) Angélique

Maintenant, faites des phrases:
par exemple: Alphonse est dans le jardin

1) Alphonse ....

2) Angélique ....

3) Alphonse ....

4) Alphonse ....

5) Angélique ....

Descriptions

Les Dutoit — troisième
Les Serre — deuxième étage
Les Heuland — premier étage
La concièrge — rez de chaussée
sous sol

Où habitent les familles dans l'immeuble?
exemple: les Heuland habitent au premier étage

2. Les Serre ....

3. Les Dutoit ....

4. La concièrge ....

à coté (de)
à droite (de)
à gauche (de)
en face (de)
au bout du couloir

A l'aide des expressions ci-dessus, décrivez l'appartement des Serre.

exemple: La chambre de M. et Mme Serre est à droite de l'entrée.

La chambre de Natasha est ....
La salle de bains est ....
La cuisine est ....
La salle à manger est ....
Le séjour est ....
Les WC sont ....
La chambre de Natasha est .... la chambre de ses parents.

Alun School's booklet

Several schools noticed that pupils appreciated getting a genuine, personal response to their questions, and felt a sense of 'ownership' when the language at their disposal was personalised and went beyond the confines of their textbook.

Croesyceiliog School organised a very successful year-long competition for its Year 7 students, the aim being for them to find out as much as possible about their Foreign Language Assistant. They made use of all the question forms learnt, and were stretched by the responses, which extended their vocabulary. This was probably the pupils' first experience of using the foreign language for a genuine communicative purpose.

Notre assistante française

1 Détails personnels
Nom
Age
Anniversaire
Domicile
Autres détails

2. Famille
Parents
Frères/soeurs
Animaux
Autres informations

3 Passetemps
Sports
Weekend
Clubs
Autres informations

Croesyceiliog School

Departmental Discussion Point

Consider the following points arising from Section 1 of this report

- *Do your pupils show independence in their oral work? Does your department employ the technique of 'progressive withdrawal of support'?*
- *Are your pupils equipped with 'communication repair strategies' early on in the language-learning process?*
- *Are your pupils given opportunities to progress to more creative/imaginative/ open-ended work?*
- *How can you differentiate the levels of support given to pupils?*
- *Are your pupils using more complex language/ showing greater fluency as they progress into KS4? (Refer to the NC levels for Attainment Target 2 as a checklist).*

Other teachers used 'mystery guests' as interviewees for KS4 pupils, who were surprised to find that there were fluent French speakers in unexpected departments of their schools, and that even more unexpectedly, these teachers had rather interesting lives outside school!

All schools who tried this more open-ended type of work found that pupils had to be equipped with 'communication repair strategies' or with a visual stimulus which might be withdrawn after a period of practice (the OHP being a particularly useful tool here). Giving pupils a time limit also served to focus their minds and avoided time-wasting when undertaking tasks such as information-gap exercises.

Several schools also discovered that eliciting the longer response can be fun, as for example at *Pembroke School*, where pupils played games such as 'Extending the Sentence'. Small groups would sit in a circle, and the first pupil would say a word or short sentence. The next pupil would have to repeat the utterance and add to it.

Pupil reaction to such games was universally positive, bringing comments such as *'I like speaking because it's the most fun thing to do'*, and *'Speaking Spanish is cool'!*

Confidence, creativity and pupil enjoyment

Several schools decided that low pupil motivation was a major problem in certain classes, and that this problem was having an adverse effect on achievement. This was particularly true in remote rural areas where trips abroad were a rare occurrence. Three schools made a particular effort to inject a greater element of fun into their language lessons, and were delighted when their efforts appeared to be bearing fruit as the project progressed.

Ysgol Alun found that **songs, raps and sketches** were particularly well received by pupils studying Welsh, as we can see from this comment from Year 9 pupil Jemma Lawrence:

'I really enjoyed making up a rap. I think it is a good way of learning because everyone in the group enjoyed the task, which made us more involved in the work and we learnt more, also the rap was helpful because when we look back on the topic I remember the rap.'

Her class-mate Louise Connelly adds:

'Blind Date was a fun and interesting way of learning Welsh. I loved acting and making the play work, especially when we had to dress up.'

A word of caution, however; although such techniques were popular in all schools involved and with the vast majority of pupils (including Year 10 boys!), they did not suit every disposition, as we see from this pupil's comment:

'I didn't mind performing the rap or writing the script, I found that fun, but I didn't like performing in front of the camera, I was embarrassed and shy, especially when the video was shown to the class.'

At *Pembroke School*, too, a small number of pupils did not gain in confidence, and found performing to be embarrassing.

Reservations apart, raps were seen to be a resounding success with pupils, teachers and Field Officers involved in the project, as they were fun, flexible and 'cool'! They also develop pupils' creativity and independence, and can build the confidence of pupils who are less eager to participate in oral work, since they are involved in a group task. The text of a rap can of course be exploited as an extension activity, and the work of a French 'rapper' like MC Solaar could even repay close study at a more advanced level.

Departmental Discussion Point
Do your pupils enjoy songs, games and raps? Could they play a more prominent role in your teaching?

- Topics covered in raps included giving your age ('*Cuantos años tiene*?'), expressing likes and dislikes about football teams ('*Liverpool, Everton, Leeds, y pêl-droed gorau yn y byd*!'— the best football in the world!), pop music and hobbies. There is really no limit to the topics which can be set to a beat and made into a 'rap'!

The evidence from *Pembroke, Alun* and *Gwendraeth* schools strongly suggests that greater enjoyment leads to increased motivation and eventually to improved pupil performance.

Use of Video

If pupils are to be recorded speaking, presenting and acting sketches on video, then there is obviously a great deal of creative work that needs to be done prior to filming. *Darland School* found that preparations for their *télémagazine* were enjoyable and motivating for the group involved and had the fortunate side-effect of improving their reading and writing skills. The teacher notes:

'Much of the research and preparation had to be done at home. The main feature of this was establishing scenarios and writing scripts. Most pupils dealt well with this aspect, enjoying the planning stage and working together in groups and pairs with great success.'

Producing a video in the classroom

As with the creative work undertaken in *Gwendraeth School*, pupil feedback was extremely positive, and showed how the skill of speaking was not improved in isolation:

'The range I can now use in my speech has inspired me to be more imaginative in my written work . . . I think the course has given me more confidence in my speaking. I have now spoken in a bigger group where mistakes were quickly dismissed and learnt from.'

All schools who used the project to build up towards a performance of some kind reported that great benefits were reaped from allowing pupils a measure of autonomy in their work. The preparatory phase was marked by enthusiasm, imagination and a willingness to work in groups. A competitive spirit could also be harnessed to produce work of a higher standard, as groups tried their best to out-perform each other!

T 4/6 *Aufgabe c2, Schülerbuch, Seite 60*

Selbstbewertung – wie bist du? Füll diese Tabelle aus:

Ich denke, ich bin ...		
sehr nett ☐	ziemlich nett ☐	nicht nett ☐
sehr gemein ☐	ziemlich gemein ☐	nicht gemein ☐
sehr faul ☐	ziemlich faul ☐	nicht faul ☐
sehr unfreundlich ☐	ziemlich unfreundlich ☐	nicht unfreundlich ☐
sehr groß ☐	ziemlich groß ☐	nicht groß ☐
sehr sportlich ☐	ziemlich sportlich ☐	nicht sportlich ☐
sehr lustig ☐	ziemlich lustig ☐	nicht lustig ☐
sehr schlank ☐	ziemlich schlank ☐	nicht schlank ☐

✂ -

T 4/6 *Aufgabe c2, Schülerbuch, Seite 60*

Ich denke,		
sehr nett ☐	ziemlich nett ☐	nicht nett ☐
sehr gemein ☐	ziemlich gemein ☐	nicht gemein ☐
sehr faul ☐	ziemlich faul ☐	nicht faul ☐
sehr unfreundlich ☐	ziemlich unfreundlich ☐	nicht unfreundlich ☐
sehr groß ☐	ziemlich groß ☐	nicht groß ☐
sehr sportlich ☐	ziemlich sportlich ☐	nicht sportlich ☐
sehr lustig ☐	ziemlich lustig ☐	nicht lustig ☐
sehr schlank ☐	ziemlich schlank ☐	nicht schlank ☐

Here is an example of a useful exercise from 'Alle einsteigen!' (Hodder & Stoughton) which was used successfully at Croesyceiliog School.

Another reported benefit of greater pupil autonomy was that pupils felt a greater sense of 'ownership' of the language, customising expressions learnt or read for their own use. Simple structured pairwork to encourage pupils to express their opinions led to a readiness to make more spontaneous comments in future work.

One can imagine such language being re-cycled by pupils in a sketch or a lengthy description which could be captured on video. *Amman Valley School* noted that their pupils were beginning to analyse their performance on video more critically, paying attention to good/poor pronunciation, grammatical errors, use of tenses and so on.

Being Involved

A surprising number of schools reported the positive effect for both staff and pupils of being involved in a 'prestigious' project. Pupils reacted favourably to the fact that their progress was being monitored (both by teachers and Field Officers) and responded well to the challenge of focusing on a skill area which they were trying to improve. Several schools conducted surveys on pupil attitudes towards speaking, with the majority of pupils responding positively, noting that it was perhaps the most useful skill of all both in their studies and for later life. Some pupils even commented that although the oral component was worth 25% of the marks at GCSE level, they did not feel that they were dedicating a proportional amount of time to it.

One of the most ambitious and creative ways of involving pupils in the learning process was seen at *Gwendraeth School*, where a whole 'community' was created for pupils to interact with. Teachers, sixth formers, FLAs and pupils were asked to develop roles (e.g. shopkeeper or hotel receptionist) and personalities, and other pupils were asked to interview them and find out as much as possible about their lives. Pupils therefore had to elicit a wide range of information, including details about work, family, home, opinions and so on. Much of this oral work was then written up for homework, with more advanced students even writing a 'history' of the village and the legends surrounding it.

Finally, although statistics are to be treated with caution, it is interesting to note the results of the *Gwendraeth* survey of pupil attitudes to their work. At the beginning of the year, 80% of pupils said they enjoyed 'acting' in the foreign language, but 55% wanted to be able to use their books as props. At the end of the year, the number enjoying acting had gone up to 95%, whilst 75% of pupils did not want to use their books at all. Like Vic Reeves, you may think that '82.5% of statistics are made up on the spot' but these figures do seem to provide very clear evidence of the project's success, especially as regards pupil confidence, creativity and enjoyment.

Departmental Discussion Point

- *Could pupils at your school benefit from the 'project' approach, whereby speaking skills become the focus of attention for a set period?*
- *How might video be used in your department to enhance oral work?*
- *Do you still employ 'fun' activities in Key Stage 4?*
- *Are your pupils provided with sufficient opportunities to speak in class, including pair and group work?*

Fluency versus Accuracy — are they mutually exclusive?

A number of schools noted that although pupils gained in confidence and fluency during the year, this improvement was not always reflected in the accuracy of their speech or in their pronunciation, which remained heavily influenced by their mother tongue. Some schools categorised this as a 'failure', and cited examples as evidence:

However well they 'knew' the various structures, the majority of pupils still seemed to throw accuracy to the winds when involved in a more complex task i.e.: one where they were concentrating on the content of what they were saying rather than on the form of the sentence. They confused one tense with another, used the infinitive inappropriately, mixed up j'ai and je suis when using the perfect, etc.

Another teacher's comment, whilst acknowledging the problem of poor pronunciation, gives a clue as to how an improvement might be achieved:

'Some pupils, through practice and perseverance (and natural flair) did manage to come very close to the ideal. In these cases, presentations were superb and inspiring to others. Often, though, scripts were used too frequently as prompts— accents left much to be desired!'

Amman Valley School's experience showed that a number of techniques can be used to reduce pupils' reliance on the written word, including:

- OHP pictures or flashcards left in view after drilling as a reminder of language being used;
- key words on notepads (especially useful when conducting surveys);
- folding pages to cover up useful questions after a timed practice period;
- picture or graphic prompts as in the new GCSE role-plays;
- providing a worksheet with full phrases/sentences on one side and a graphic representation of them on the other.

Croesyceiliog School felt that a more structured grammatical/linguistic progression must underpin their pupils' oral work, thus making learners aware of the structures which they can adapt and manipulate as they speak. By listening carefully to a question, for example, it may be possible to re-use some of the language in the reply. Some question forms may lead naturally to a set reply (e.g. *Pourquoi*? . . . *Parce que* . . .). The teachers revised their scheme of work with this aim in mind, and tried to ensure that progression was not merely a question of a change of topic — language as well as content should move on and build on what had been learnt previously.

Departmental Discussion Point

- *Are your pupils aware of the 'criteria for success' in speaking?*
- *What is your policy on error correction during oral work?*
- *How confident do your pupils feel about speaking? (Are they afraid of making mistakes?)*

Many schools set listening homework based on a cassette provided, but it is also possible to use the same taped material as pronunciation practice, or to set 'oral homework' where pupils must prepare a short exposé based on a taped model. These ideas were used successfully in some project schools, and brought good results in terms of improved pronunciation and fluency.

The simple worksheet below from *Croesyceiliog School* prompted pupils to conduct a survey, which gave them an opportunity to speak to a wide range of class-mates. At the same time, however, they were being made to drill verb forms and question forms.

This activity was followed up by the question '*Wer geht gern schwimmen?*' in a conscious effort to make pupils aware of different verb forms which they gradually learnt to manipulate.

Lewis Girls' School found that the pupils responded well when they were given the criteria for success in speaking. Their oral work was sometimes assessed/commented on in class, or pairs of girls recorded their efforts on tape for assessment at a later time.

The criteria for success were:

- **communication (always seen as central);**
- **pronunciation;**
- **accuracy;**
- **fluency;**
- **initiative / sustaining flow.**

These criteria (or very similar ones) are a feature of GCSE and 'A' Level syllabuses throughout Wales and England, and it seems only fair that pupils be made aware of them. Other schools made posters exemplifying the eight National Curriculum Levels of Achievement, which again provided learners with a yardstick to measure their own progress.

By setting appropriate goals for learners and raising our expectations of what can be achieved in oral work, we may yet achieve a greater degree of fluency without 'throwing accuracy to the winds'.

Topic Aa: The Language of the Classroom

You must be able :....

1. to greet and address someone appropriately in the language
   Guten Morgen Frau M....! Guten Tag, Herr E......! Wie geht's Ihnen?
   Tag Peter! Wie geht's (dir)? Hallo! Tschüs!

2. to state whether or not something is understood
   Ich verstehe nicht. Ich habe das nicht (richtig) verstanden.

3. to ask for something to be repeated
   Wie bitte? Noch einmal bitte!
   Können Sie das bitte wiederholen?

4. to spell and to ask how something is spelt
   Wie schreibt [buchstabiert] man das / das Wort ...X...?

5. to ask what things are called in German
   Wie heißt das auf Deutsch? Wie sagt man ...... auf Deutsch?

6. to ask someone to speak more slowly
   Können Sie bitte langsamer sprechen?

7. to ask for explanation, clarification and help
   Können Sie das mir bitte erklären?
   Was bedeutet.........?
   Können Sie mir bitte helfen?

8. to make apologies
   Entschuldigung. Verzeihung. Es tut mir leid.

9. to ask if something is correct
   Ist das richtig?

10. to ask permission to do things
    Darf ich ....?

11. to say which languages they speak and comment on how well they speak them
    Ich spreche Deutsch und Französisch
    Ich kann ... X ... [sehr/ziemlich/nicht sehr/nicht besonders] gut sprechen

12. to state languages they would like to learn and give reasons
    Ich möchte Spanisch / Russisch / Italienisch / Japanisch lernen.
    Ich möchte in Spanien arbeiten und wohnen. Ich möchte viel reisen!
    Meine Familie stammt aus Italien, und ich möchte diese Sprache lernen.
    Ich fahre gern in Urlaub, und lerne gern Fremdsprachen.

13. to ask whether someone speaks a particular language
    Sprechen Sie/ Sprichst du ..X..?

14. to say how long they have been studying the language
    Ich lerne Deutsch / Französisch seit vier / fünf Jahren

Croesyceiliog (German) worksheet

Chapter Three

Teachers and teaching

•Mike Clarke

In the previous chapter, the characteristics, elements and progression of pupils' speaking abilities have been examined. What the pupils achieved was undoubtedly impressive, but what enabled them to make the linguistic strides they did? Their teachers: their willingness to be part of the Project and their commitment to it.

How did the Project teachers create spontaneity and motivation develop confidence and fluency and enhance pupils' whole speaking experience? The first part of this chapter sets the context within which the various approaches and strategies were adopted; in the second, the spotlight turns upon the particular techniques employed.

(i) Setting the Context

The schools were asked to take part in action research and that involved taking risks. Many activities were new to the teachers concerned or pushed beyond previous (safe) limits. In other cases, a combination of linguistic objectives, deemed too ambitious before, were successfully achieved. Teachers gradually allowed pupils to take the initiative and develop impetus. As with all action research, some things worked, others didn't. That did not matter: what mattered was pushing the boundaries, trying things new to that teacher or department. The successes were impressive, outstandingly so at times, and far outweighed the less successful activities. Where teachers breached previous perimeters and pupils grew in confidence and motivation, so the contexts for speaking were extended, broadened, deepened.

Given that the crucial element in the Project was to increase and improve pupils' use of the target language, it was essential that teachers always, or almost always, used it themselves. Although it is the single, most important requirement of the National Curriculum, teachers still re-assessed their own use of the target language. All were clearly committed to it anyway, but many found areas where they were able to increase their target language use and thereby encourage their pupils to see it as the norm. This included not only all aspects of communication within the classroom but outside it too; in fact, wherever pupils might hear their teachers, especially when talking to each other.

It became immediately clear that establishing the right atmosphere in the classroom was vital. In the recent survey on *Speaking Skills in Modern Foreign Languages*, HMI commented on

good teachers' classrooms: '*an encouraging atmosphere, in which pupils were unafraid to make mistakes and in which a sense of enjoyment was evident.*' The bane of the language teacher for decades has been the reluctance of pupils (and adults!) to speak for fear of making a mistake, of not 'getting it completely right'. Teachers, therefore, made a conscious effort to banish fear, to convince pupils that making mistakes does not matter but that having a go does. This led many teachers to considerably alter their approaches to correction, often reviewing and re-drawing departmental policies. Instead of criticising any wrong utterance, teachers were far more tolerant of mistakes than they might have been in order to encourage participation and extended speaking. HMI recommends this approach: '*Care is taken not to interrupt the flow of pupils' language, and the teacher by no means corrects every error.*'

Once a non-threatening atmosphere was established, teachers strove to make the activities fun. This, of course, does not just happen: there are not inconsiderable planning implications. However, it became abundantly clear both to teachers and Field Officers that, where activities were both clearly focused and hugely enjoyable, pupils' motivation aptly demonstrated the old adage that nothing succeeds like success. Motivation built confidence which was reflected in growing competence and fluency (though, as is discussed elsewhere, not always with accent and accuracy). Increased competence created more enjoyment, and so on. All the participating schools bore witness to this, reason enough to enthuse anyone. Pupils particularly enjoy speaking when they are active at the same time. Teachers, therefore, developed activities where the pupils do things. This ranged from throwing the bean-bag (*Alun*), running to a wall or board (Pembroke), moving around the Eurovillage (*Gwendraeth*) to acting sketches and performing songs in public (*Darland*, *Maelor* and *Mynyddbach*).

An area allied to physical activity is competition. The competitive instinct is always very strong in children, and teachers exploited this astutely via team games, a points scored log and league tables. The *Gladiators* game, described in part two of this chapter, was an exciting example. Similarly, pupils are blessed with vivid imaginations, the fruits of which were often harvested. The resulting 'ownership' of the activity by the pupils produced its own motivation.

'*A significant factor . . . is the predominance of whole class oral work. . . . If other strategies are not also employed, most pupils actually speak little in class, and some hardly at all.*' (HMI Survey). Taking up this point, many teachers involved in the Project specifically designed strategies to ensure that when oral work was being carried out all pupils were involved to the maximum. Similarly, there was an awareness that too much of too many lessons was teacher led. Teachers resolved to stand back, to give some control for learning to the pupils. As the latter responded positively to being allowed the initiative, learner control was increased. Results were almost always extremely encouraging, sometimes dramatically so as pupils themselves pushed the boundaries of their vocabulary, language structure and expression. HMI had noted that where teaching is good, there was '*a high level of participation by all or most pupils.*' Teachers have often found it difficult to step back, to relinquish a measure of control, but if pupils are to maximise their speaking skills, the Project has shown this to be essential. Allied to learner control is self-assessment which is dealt with in the next section. Suffice to say here that when the criteria for good performance are clearly explained to them, pupils assess their own and their peers' efforts with perception and maturity.

As with all good teaching, the expectations teachers had of their pupils were high but realistic. Confidence grew, fluency developed and the length of utterances increased. However, just about all the schools reported negative side effects which, as adult learners have also experienced, appear to be part of the complex learning process. Accuracy, accent and pronunciation often suffered. As the pupils concentrated on the length and content of what they were saying, so the form, sound and structure of how they said it were 'thrown to the winds' as one teacher put it. As an example of good expectations, the HMI Survey said: '*Pupils are encouraged and expected to speak in sentences rather than monosyllables, and teachers do not accept simple or short sentences from pupils who are capable of longer or more complex utterances.*' But, as regards teaching approaches, HMI went on to say: '*Pupils are trained to speak with good pronunciation and accent.*' What the Project has indicated is that fluency and accuracy do not necessarily go together. As a counter to this, some of the teachers took language that had been worked on and led sessions which specifically concentrated on pronunciation or accuracy alone. The next time pupils used that language, there was a definite improvement. It is an area that clearly calls for close monitoring.

Many of the schools reported, at least initially, that those pupils who were deriving most benefit from the Project were the more able. Less able pupils were often much more reluctant to be involved. Teachers felt that they needed to be specifically prepared for this. However, as time went on, lower-ability pupils became encouraged by the example of their classmates. This was particularly effective in pairs or groups of mixed ability levels.

Just as pupils performed better in drama situations once they got rid of their scripts, so they thought and spoke more for themselves as written visual support was taken away or reduced. Much work on this was done in Amman Valley where the linguistic structures needed for any given activity were gradually withdrawn. At the same time, written vocabulary was progressively replaced by headings, pictures and symbols. Quite complex surveys were eventually carried out without a single supporting written word. Similar work was carried out in Abersychan, Croesyceiliog and in David Hughes where cue cards were used to encourage longer verbal exchanges.

Teachers developed the presence and use of wall charts and mobiles. It was clear that such support materials needed to be easily within the pupils' vision. Posters bearing target language expressions for pupil use were made big and bold; once in place, their use was insisted on.

In some classrooms the target language was accompanied by the English equivalent or an explanatory diagram or drawing. One school specifically targeted 'repair' or coping strategies aimed at helping pupils to keep going when communication broke down. Where more than one language is taught in the same room, pupils are easily confused if there is no clear division between those languages. Some teachers decided to split the classroom and have one language on each side, others used a colour coding scheme whereby each language would have its own colour — simple but effective.

While some lessons were conducted in traditionally arranged classrooms, in order to allow pupils to be active and move about (which had a marked effect in reducing inhibitions), teachers thought carefully about their classroom organisation. This concerned both the physical layout of the room and also the composition of pupil groupings. The creation of space for the pupils to prepare and perform in was a marked feature of the work in Abersychan and Mynyddbach.

The whole business of foreign language teaching, other than in situ, relies heavily on the pupils' 'willing suspension of disbelief'. It was no surprise, then, to read the enthusiastic comments of the youngsters and to see the clear motivation from being in realistic situations. Some schools made imaginative use of their own environment: school yard, dining hall, headteacher's office and so on. The most ambitious project in this respect was at Gwendraeth where a whole 'Eurovillage' was created in a disused space. With generous funding and in-school help the 'village' was built, comprising café, bank, market stalls, clothes shop, railway station, hotel tourist office and cinema. The teachers had to learn how to handle groups of pupils in the 'village' and early work was straightforward and transactional. As both teachers' and pupils' enthusiasm grew and imagination developed, scenarios similarly expanded their linguistic horizons. Unexpected events took place and pupils found themselves relating a robbery or kidnapping to the police and describing someone who had left without paying. Staff, assistants and sixth formers took on identities as villagers and pupils had to interview them about their work and life in the village. Clearly, the Eurovillage is an enormous advantage and the pupils love being in it. However, every classroom and school are susceptible to encouraging the development of ideas and acting as a mirror to reality in a similar, if less grand, way.

Schools that were using drama techniques allowed pupils to use props and wear costumes. This applied to playing characters in sketches, being television presenters or pretending to be on a train or in a hospital. There is no doubt that this increased the pupils' motivation and, consequently, their desire to perform well in the language.

All the foregoing meant that it was no surprise that pupils were very keen to perform to an audience. Their pride in performance and in the standard and accuracy of what they said, sang or rapped was eloquent testimony to the effectiveness of this approach. Every teacher is encouraged to video their pupils. Even when just discussing their language studies or chatting generally, as cited in the previous section, pupils 'upped' their performance considerably once they were on camera. The same applied in those cases where pupils performed at a school eisteddfod.

Often because the pupils themselves were wanting to extend their powers of expression, a number of teachers felt the need to teach grammar to enable this to happen. It was interesting that this judicious teaching of grammar arose from the fact that pupils had a measure of linguistic initiative.

(ii) Techniques Employed

Having set the context for the approaches adopted by teachers, this section now looks at some of the particular techniques employed. Inevitably, those items mentioned are but a small selection of the myriad activities that went on in the project classes during the course of the year. They do represent, however, a bank of ideas that were successfully put into practice. There were, of course, many variations on a theme across the twelve schools; the activities, therefore, are exemplars and are susceptible to almost infinite adaptation by teachers to suit the differing circumstances of their classes.

There are a multitude of activities to encourage pupils to speak which will regularly occur in language classrooms. If these are not mentioned in depth, it is only because the teachers involved in the Project were also trying to push beyond what they had done before. Flashcards were still used, as were grids, boxes, tick lists, etc. Pelmanism featured regularly and imaginative use was made of OHTs. Surveys were an important element, (included in the comments on good teaching practice in the recent *Speaking Skills in Modern Foreign Languages* by HMI: '*Those departments in which speaking is best developed . . . create regular opportunities, through small group work, pair activities, or surveys, for many pupils to talk at the same time*).'

As HMI noted, successful teaching gives frequent opportunities for pupils to use the target language, usually including pair and group work. Much of the work described in this section involves pair and group work in some form or other, clearly vital in the attempt to maximise pupils' speaking development. At its simplest level, teachers always tried to ensure that communication involved a genuine information gap. This becomes more successful when '*support (usually written) . . . is gradually withdrawn*' (HMI). One simple activity mentioned by HMI was where pupils were either 'A' or 'B'. The 'A' pupils remained seated while the 'Bs' moved along one space at each signal from the teacher. This ensured that pupils did not just have a dialogue with their friends but optimised pupil contact.

One of the main aims for many teachers was to increase the amount of time pupils spent asking, as opposed to just answering, questions and to enhance their ability to do so. In Lewis School, for example, teachers would hold challenge sessions where pupils would see how many different questions they could come up with in a given amount of time.

Alun School incorporated 'commercial breaks' into their lessons during which pupils were allowed to chat about anything they wanted - provided they did so in the target language.

Games usually offer a sure-fire way of holding pupils' attention, particularly as a means of motivating the reluctant. Simple board games and cards were successfully used. In Pembroke, teachers devised a whole series of action games, usually against the clock. Scrabble was not only played but the pupils made their own boards. Dice offered many possibilities; not only number dice but also those with letters, colours, words or verbs. Two or more different types of dice were successfully used in combination to create sentences such as: *'J'ai acheté, quatre pulls bleus'*. One school used the competitive spirit with a game called *Gladiators*. Each member of one team held a card and formed a corridor through which, in turn, each member of the other team had to run the gauntlet, saying something about each card. Points could be scored or each runner timed and the totals added up. Pupils still enjoyed the challenge of popular activities such as the one where a group of pupils are in a circle and each person has to repeat what has already been said and add something else. The first person might say *'Je porte une chemise blanche,'* the second *'Je porte une chemise blanche et une cravate rouge'* and so on. Adding different comments all starting with the same letter went down well with older pupils e.g. *'Je m'appelle Michel, j'habite . . . Marseille et j'aime la marmelade.'*

It is well known that music and rhythm are great aids to memory. Songs were used in a variety of ways, especially at KS3. The aversion to singing at KS4 is well documented but raps were amazingly successful with all age groups, including boys. Pupils in many classes enjoyed developing their own raps immensely and were prepared to work very hard at it. Also, 'scripts' were soon dispensed with in order to facilitate the accompanying actions. Other teachers used songs to drill structures such as daily routine, the perfect tense, German prepositional use; these were supported by pictures on the OHP.

Not surprisingly, perhaps the most spectacular results arose from the use of drama. In fact, in some of the Project schools, the whole emphasis rested on the exploitation of 'performance' in some form or other. Teachers encouraged pupils to collaborate in the writing of scripts for role-plays which then extended into open-ended drama, supported by props and costumes. Pupils were offered the opportunity to write and perform their own sketches on the theme of 'boy meets girl'. TV quizzes and game shows such as *Blockbusters*, *The Price is Right* and, of course, *Blind Date* were accepted with enthusiasm, recalling those ever-popular presentations at Language Festivals. Maelor School used the *Alphonse* strip cartoons in *Route Nationale* as the basis for much work. Pupils took on the identities of characters in the cartoon and answered personal information questions, thus integrating a number of skills. Pupils rehearsed and performed the *Alphonse* sketches, then adapted them to fit their own personae and situations. These were subsequently performed at the school eisteddfod. Other schools made various uses of other identities, real or imagined, for a range of 'Who am I?' activities.

In Darland, teachers guided pupils into creating their own television magazine programme called 'Télémag'. They found useful ideas in the *In-Play* materials. The eventual 'programme' included advertisements, agony aunt, fashion, features (e.g. healthy eating), horoscopes, interviews, news, personal presentations, problems (e.g. smoking), recipes, reviews, sketches and spotlight on Chester. Impressive!

Real life can be as interesting as make-believe in the right circumstances. Amman Valley set up a video-conference link with another school and pupils who did not know each other at all had to find out as much information about each other as possible. This was a brave experiment which threw up technical and social challenges as well as linguistic. It was certainly an activity worth pursuing and persevering with.

A message board was made available for pupils to put up any messages, personal or 'official', in the target language. This met with mixed success, being used mainly by the more able pupils. Teachers were considering extending the idea to a graffiti board where pupils could write any reasonable comments, provided at least some of the message was in the target language.

More active use of wall displays was targeted. One wall had coloured bands on it with the relevant French names; another had question words accompanied by explanatory pictures. On the matter of colours, in Lewis and other schools, different genders on word posters were allotted different colours: a simple but effective mnemonic.

AT1 and AT2 are naturally interdependent and many teachers made frequent use of listening exercises to act as models for speaking. Glan Ely found the Language Master provided valuable assistance. One school had an interesting listening activity where the teacher gave directions to and descriptions of countries in Europe which the pupils had to identify.

The value of reading aloud was not forgotten either. With the help of the foreign language assistant, pupils practised by reading their readers out loud.

Speaking was used with verbs by taking an idea and moving it through the tenses e.g. *je vais manger, je mange, j'ai mangé.*

In the attempt to banish English from the classroom, Croesyceiliog had rubbish bins fixed to the wall. Every time a pupil spoke in English, the utterance was written down and thrown in the bin. It proved effective because pupils did not want their words to end up there. Other classrooms had 'language policemen' who noted any use of English and for which sanctions were imposed, for example, the docking of team points.

Language Bins

Departmental Discussion Point
— focusing on speaking

The following elements discussed in this chapter could provide a useful tick-list for departments when preparing the ground for a speaking skills project.

- Action research means taking risks: extend the context.
- Use the target language.
- Create a non-threatening atmosphere; banish fear. Attitude to error correction?
- Make it fun; let the pupils be active.
- Use the competitive instinct.
- Allow learner control; make lessons less teacher led.
- High but realistic expectations. Beware accent, accuracy and pronunciation.
- Appropriate support for the less able.
- Gradually withdraw written support (worksheets, OHTs, etc.).
- Language posters, etc, prominently displayed.
- Classroom organisation: 'fitness for purpose'.
- Mirror reality: use real settings; create a realistic setting.
- Use props and costumes.
- Provide an audience: video pupils; eisteddfod.
- Grammar: demand may be pupil led.

Chapter Four

Assessment and merit systems

•Ceri James

Why assess speaking?

If it is true that pupils become demotivated when the written work in their exercise books is not marked by their teacher for a long period of time, then the same is probably true of oral work. Pupils tend to consider that if there is no assessment, if there is no mark or feedback on an oral activity, then that activity is in some way less important than a written assignment, which is normally marked and annotated by their teacher.

In the schools which conducted surveys on pupil attitudes to speaking, it was found that pupils wanted to be assessed or given feedback on their progress. At *Gwendraeth School*, 100 per cent of pupils wanted to have their speaking assessed as much as possible in the *Eurovillage*. The school responded by making the following arrangements:

1. As a pupil carries out a task the teacher or assistant notes details of the task and a mark is given for how well the task has been carried out.
2. Worksheets are completed and other written assignments set.
3. Interviews are recorded on cassette or video for analysis in the classroom.

The teacher adds:

'Feedback and evaluation sessions have been crucial. The pupils see themselves on screen and are sometimes able to recognise and correct their own errors.'

Pupils were given the criteria for success, and consequently began to take a more active role in the assessment process, commenting on their own performance and on that of their peers.

EUROVILLAGE : AT2 SPEAKING

AU CAFÉ Niveau 1 ___ 2 ___ 3 ___ 4 ___ 5 ___ 6 ___ 7 ___ 8 ___

Nom : ___

À LA POSTE Niveau 1 ___ 2 ___ 3 ___ 4 ___ 5 ___ 6 ___ 7 ___ 8 ___

Nom : ___

À LA BANQUE Niveau 1 ___ 2 ___ 3 ___ 4 ___ 5 ___ 6 ___ 7 ___ 8 ___

EUROVILLAGE : AT2 SPEAKING

À LA GARE Niveau 1 ___ 2 ___ 3 ___ 4 ___ 5 ___ 6 ___ 7 ___ 8 ___

Nom : ___

AU CINÉMA Niveau 1 ___ 2 ___ 3 ___ 4 ___ 5 ___ 6 ___ 7 ___ 8 ___

Nom : ___

À L'HÔTEL Niveau 1 ___ 2 ___ 3 ___ 4 ___ 5 ___ 6 ___ 7 ___ 8 ___

EUROVILLAGE : AT2 SPEAKING

AU SYNDICAT D'INITIATIVE Niveau 1 ___ 2 ___ 3 ___ 4 ___ 5 ___ 6 ___ 7 ___ 8 ___

Nom : ___

AU MAGASIN DE VÊTEMENTS Niveau 1 ___ 2 ___ 3 ___ 4 ___ 5 ___ 6 ___ 7 ___ 8 ___

Nom : ___

AU MARCHÉ Niveau 1 ___ 2 ___ 3 ___ 4 ___ 5 ___ 6 ___ 7 ___ 8 ___

Gwendraeth assessment sheet

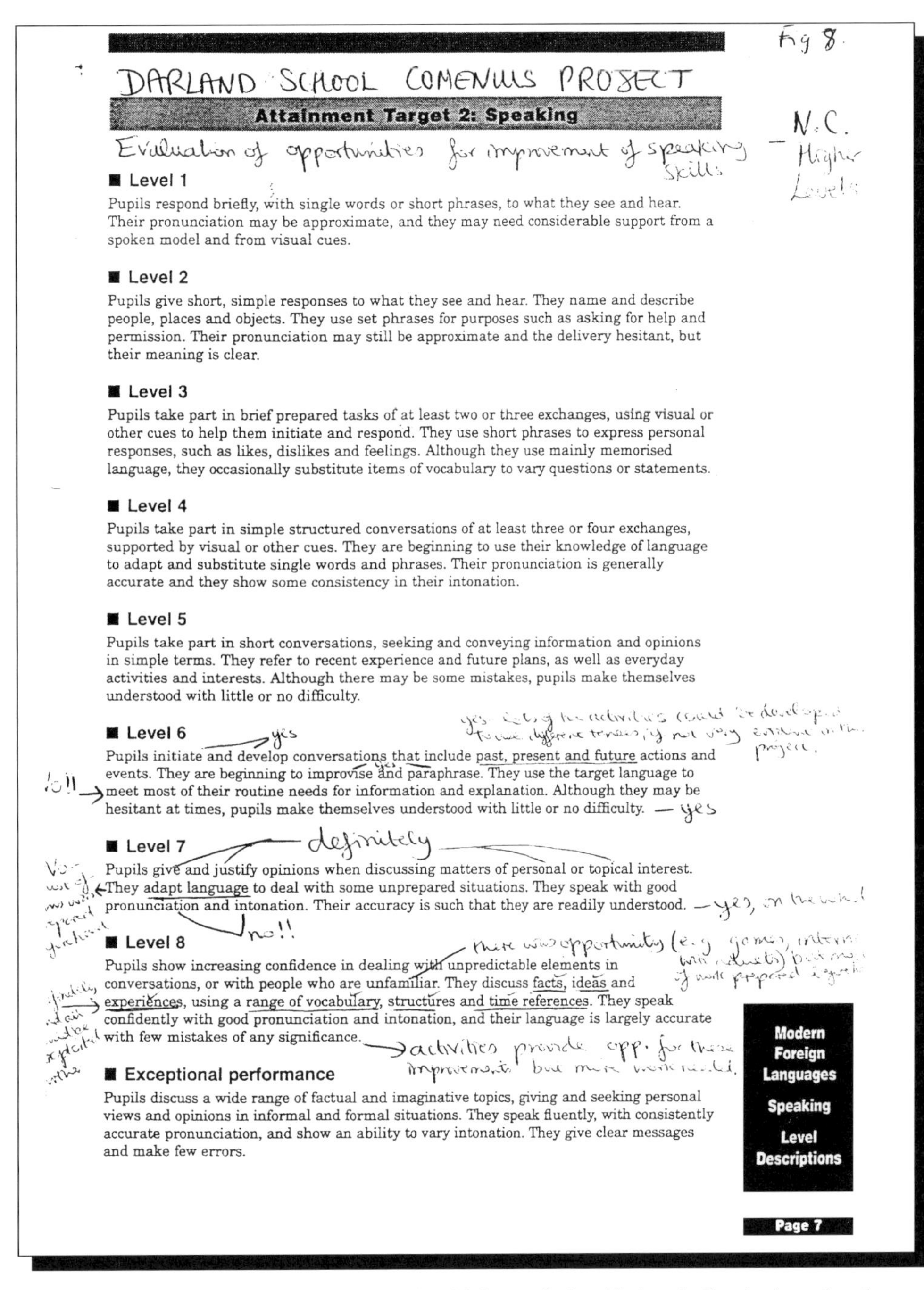

Fig 8.

DARLAND SCHOOL COMENIUS PROJECT

Attainment Target 2: Speaking

Evaluation of opportunities for improvement of speaking skills

N.C. – Higher Levels

■ **Level 1**

Pupils respond briefly, with single words or short phrases, to what they see and hear. Their pronunciation may be approximate, and they may need considerable support from a spoken model and from visual cues.

■ **Level 2**

Pupils give short, simple responses to what they see and hear. They name and describe people, places and objects. They use set phrases for purposes such as asking for help and permission. Their pronunciation may still be approximate and the delivery hesitant, but their meaning is clear.

■ **Level 3**

Pupils take part in brief prepared tasks of at least two or three exchanges, using visual or other cues to help them initiate and respond. They use short phrases to express personal responses, such as likes, dislikes and feelings. Although they use mainly memorised language, they occasionally substitute items of vocabulary to vary questions or statements.

■ **Level 4**

Pupils take part in simple structured conversations of at least three or four exchanges, supported by visual or other cues. They are beginning to use their knowledge of language to adapt and substitute single words and phrases. Their pronunciation is generally accurate and they show some consistency in their intonation.

■ **Level 5**

Pupils take part in short conversations, seeking and conveying information and opinions in simple terms. They refer to recent experience and future plans, as well as everyday activities and interests. Although there may be some mistakes, pupils make themselves understood with little or no difficulty.

■ **Level 6** — yes

Pupils initiate and develop conversations that include past, present and future actions and events. They are beginning to improvise and paraphrase. They use the target language to meet most of their routine needs for information and explanation. Although they may be hesitant at times, pupils make themselves understood with little or no difficulty. — yes

■ **Level 7** — definitely

Pupils give and justify opinions when discussing matters of personal or topical interest. They adapt language to deal with some unprepared situations. They speak with good pronunciation and intonation. Their accuracy is such that they are readily understood. — yes, on the whole

no!!

■ **Level 8**

Pupils show increasing confidence in dealing with unpredictable elements in conversations, or with people who are unfamiliar. They discuss facts, ideas and experiences, using a range of vocabulary, structures and time references. They speak confidently with good pronunciation and intonation, and their language is largely accurate with few mistakes of any significance. → activities provide opp. for these improvements but more work needed.

■ **Exceptional performance**

Pupils discuss a wide range of factual and imaginative topics, giving and seeking personal views and opinions in informal and formal situations. They speak fluently, with consistently accurate pronunciation, and show an ability to vary intonation. They give clear messages and make few errors.

Modern Foreign Languages

Speaking

Level Descriptions

Page 7

Simple assessment sheets were developed which used the National Curriculum levels to monitor pupil performance in each of the 'units' of the *Eurovillage*.

Darland School, too, found that referring back to the NC levels provided a useful measure of progress, as we see from the annotated copy above.

The Head of Department felt that this type of assessment was more 'low-key' and less intrusive, given that the pupils were actively involved in producing a video. The evidence of progress was nevertheless clearly there, and helped to allay any fears about the validity of spending so much time on the video project.

Different forms of assessment

Pupils were assessed in a variety of different ways in the project schools, and it was interesting to note the approaches which were developed to suit local needs. At *Pembroke School*, where low pupil motivation had been identified as a problem, the department changed its approach to assessment ('*We now assess less formally and more often*') and decided to introduce a **Merit System**.

The merit system involved the distribution of stars, stickers and merit certificates for good oral work. In this way, small achievements were rewarded immediately, but were also 'banked' towards a more substantial reward, which might be awarded at the end of term. The departmental system was also designed to feed into the school's own merit system.

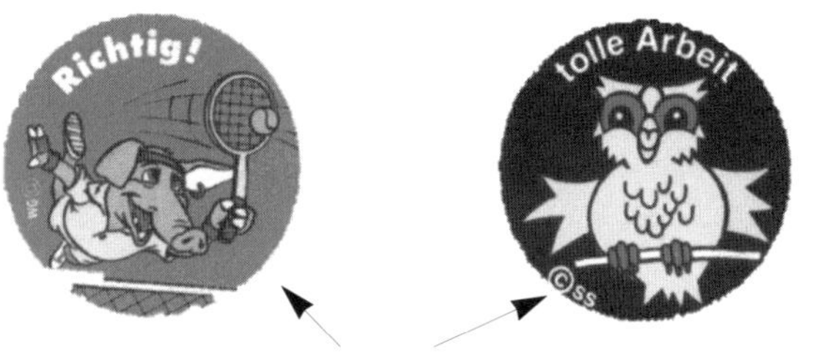

Merit stickers

The Head of Department explains:

'Our rewards system, whereby a pupil had a tick placed against his/her name after saying something in the target language (eventually to be accumulated for a monetary prize) promoted healthy competition . . . points scoring games and timed activities were very successful for this reason. Pupils were also very keen to assess their peers, and entered into this task with enthusiasm and a surprising amount of professionalism.'

This shows that monitoring of pupils' speaking can take many forms, and that use of games or peer assessment can also be incorporated into an assessment scheme.

What do we do next?

1. Ensure that momentum continues.
2. Make sure that all the classroom posters for support in TL are displayed in each room consistent with our new guidelines. That they are translated into all 3 MFLs. Find strategies for gradually withdrawing the support as pupils progress within the language.
3. Spend time planning/modifying the schemes for work for Year 7 and 9 to include our new strategies and teaching ethos.
4. Use the OHP roll — it will mean spending time to save time.
5. Work together throughout the department to ensure consistency in planning and delivery.
6. Extend the Merit system to include badges/personalised stamps/more pupil friendly rewards.
7. Continue to brainstorm to produce new and imaginative ideas for games and tasks.
8. Develop those ideas which this year never really got off the ground (for whatever reason) e.g. the idea of the Language Police, which in this school is probably more suited to Year 7 pupils.
9. Continue to review our assessment procedures and rewrite the guidelines for staff in the Department Handbook.

11. Spend the CILT money!

Other schools also introduced merit schemes which gave short term rewards for good oral work, and *Croesyceiliog School* found that an amusing form of 'punishment' could also prove motivating for pupils. They fixed a 'poubelle' or 'Mülleimer' to the classroom wall, and if pupils said anything in English it was written on a scrap of paper and consigned to the dustbin! (see previous chapter). Pupils could 'empty' the dustbin by redeeming themselves at a later stage by speaking in the target language. At the end of the year several pupils said that this was the thing they liked most about the project!

At *Lewis Girls' School* an interesting attempt was made to bring home the importance of oral work to young pupils: in KS3 their *cahier de devoirs* (they also have a *cahier de leçons*) is organised so that the front half is for speaking and writing work and the back half for reading and listening work. On one page of the speaking section, headed *Ma Participation Orale en Classe*, they log their oral contributions to classwork. The date of the lesson is noted in the margin and the pupil then logs the teacher's positive response (*très bien*, *bravo* or something of that ilk) throughout the lesson. These are totalled at the end of the lesson and a number is decided upon whereby a pupil may gain a *Bon point* (star) that feeds into the school's merit system.

Glan Ely School also used rewards as a way of motivating children, and found that formal presentations of prizes such as dictionaries were appreciated by pupils, who increased their efforts to use the target language in class.

Creating opportunities for pupils to speak is obviously an essential first step before assessment can take place. '*Strategies must be used to ensure that for 25% of their MFL curriculum, they can practise and achieve at the skill of Speaking,*' (*Pembroke School*). Obviously if lessons are too teacher-led, and involve only teacher-pupil exchanges, then it will be very difficult to reach this target.

Once opportunities had been created for pupils to speak, **peer assessment and self-assessment** techniques were successfully employed in a number of schools, and '*pupils dealt with this in a* *far more mature way than one expected!'* (*Alun School*). These assessment techniques again involve communicating to pupils what is considered to be a good oral response, and means that they become more actively involved in the learning and assessment process. The project focused teachers' attention on monitoring progress, and several schools resolved to involve pupils more in the year ahead:

'We intend to tell the pupils what we are doing and why, to try to involve them in the whole process. They can tell us what they think works and what doesn't and we aim to encourage them to think for themselves about how they acquire strategies and develop their communicative use of the language.' (Croesyceiliog School)

Departmental Discussion Point

- *Do you operate a merit scheme? If not, might it be beneficial?*
- *Do you assess speaking regularly?*
- *Do you use the National Curriculum levels in your assessment?*
- *Are pupils made aware of the assessment criteria for oral work?*
- *Do you set 'oral homework'?*
- *Can cassette/video recorders play a part in your monitoring of pupil progress?*
- *Do you create opportunities for self-assessment?*

Several schools set up schemes to assess **oral and listening homework**, and despite the time-consuming nature of such assessment for the teacher, most considered the idea to be worth the effort. Work-saving options included:

- using the FLA to mark tapes;
- pupils working in pairs with peer assessment;
- eliciting the help of sixth form students;
- preparing an oral exposé to deliver in class.

One school invested the project grant money received in small, hand-held cassette recorders, which made oral pairwork and its assessment much more practicable. Again pupil reaction to these experiments was very positive. Others made successful use of **video** both for its motivating effect and as a means of recording and analysing pupils' performance. This analysis was carried out by both teachers and pupils, and led to a greater understanding of the improvements which teachers were striving for.

Mynyddbach School made considerable use of video, and reported that their formal assessments revealed not only a much improved oral performance in one-to-one tests, but also improved scores for reading and writing, with pupils producing lengthier items than in previous years. This was confirmed by the County Adviser for Welsh, who was impressed by the pupils' confidence during role-plays and sketches — '*They were very motivated, and were not afraid to make mistakes. They understood that this was a phase which had to be gone through to achieve communication.*'

Indeed, one of the most striking aspects in the majority of project schools was the willingness of staff to ask pupils what they thought of their lessons, how they viewed their progress, and how they thought they might improve in future. The vast majority of pupils appeared to respond well to this trust and sense of involvement, and pupil-teacher relations improved as a result.

In schools where MFL and Welsh Second Language teachers were collaborating, good tips were gleaned from colleagues, especially as 40% of the marks in GCSE Welsh are allocated to the oral component (split between individual and group work). If much of our teaching tends to be 'assessment-driven', then perhaps the example of Welsh can provide some inspiration for MFL teachers. The dialogue which has been started can only benefit both sets of language teachers.

Finally, if pupil enjoyment and motivation are important factors in improving performance, then this comment by a pupil from *Darland School* about her involvement in the video project must surely indicate that she will be approaching her GCSE examination with greater confidence :

'It was a very enjoyable activity. It involved everything I have ever learnt in French, and took a lot of time to prepare. I was worried about people forgetting what to say. Everyone had put so much time and effort into it that it went well and was enjoyed by all.'

A positive assessment indeed!

Chapter Five

Planning, organisation and support

•Mike Clarke

In the chapter covering pupils' performance and what teachers did to effect that performance, the focus has rightly been on the classroom and what happened in it. However, none of that occurred by magic but as the result of a considerable amount of preparatory time and effort. To prepare the contexts in which pupils' speaking skills developed, all schools felt the need for clear planning. It was also essential to ensure that organisation was such that planned activities enjoyed optimum conditions for success. Support mechanisms had a role to play too. Teachers pointed out that while planning took time and thought, any activity only had to be planned once.

Teachers found that being part of the Speaking Skills Project meant that they had to rethink the place of speaking in their overall planning. It quickly became apparent that the Scheme of Work (SoW) had a crucial role to play and that specific speaking activities needed to be integrated into it. It was found that putting the emphasis on Attainment Target (AT) 2 had repercussions on the other three ATs, but, in the end, it proved to be worth doing so, as all-round benefits accrued. Insisting on project activities having their place in the SoW ensures that departments work together to agree approaches and activities. Having decided on which activities to incorporate, departments then go on to work together to produce what they need. HMI, in the survey *Speaking Skills in Modern Foreign Languages*, noted that where departmental organisation was good '*Members of the department share the production of materials.*'

'*Strategies for improving speaking are discussed and planned in departmental meetings and in-service training.*' (HMI). What HMI observed as good practice was certainly echoed by the project schools. One or two people may provide the initial impetus but for all pupils to derive benefit from improved speaking skills, the preparatory work must be undertaken by the department as a whole. The need for such collaboration can determine not just the agenda for highly valuable training sessions but can also give a more purposeful edge to departmental meetings. The latter, as every teacher knows, can get bogged down in administrative matters to the exclusion of all else. This often means that departments rarely, if at all, discuss methodology. By guaranteeing time in departmental meetings for working on speaking skills, discussions are focused, ideas brainstormed, approaches shared. Departments can get down to the nitty-gritty of turning the ideas into materials, sharing the work and building up a veritable bank of materials available to all and 'owned' by all. Peer pressure creates its own momentum and helps to ensure that all teachers in a department contribute to the process in full. Once activities and materials have been tried in the classroom, then appraisal of the extent to which they have been more or less successful can be fed back into meetings. As a number of schools reported, by using meetings in this way, teachers created a system where they shared, supported and learned from each other. Lewis School found that although there is a lot of preparation initially, in the medium to long term, workload is reduced.

Not only is much to be gained by intra-departmental work, but also collaboration between departments can be a fruitful source of inspiration, ideas and techniques. Modern Foreign Languages and Welsh have much to offer each other. (In other contexts, English as a Foreign Language is a natural ally). Although Welsh will have been taught throughout KS1 and KS2, and the AT weightings are slightly different from MFL, the aim to create fluent, confident speakers is the same. In *Mynyddbach*, the Welsh and French teachers selected classes that they both taught as the Project classes. In Year 7, pupils combined the freshness of a new language (French) with the experience of having already learned Welsh for six years. There is no doubt whatever that pupils' performances and development in both languages benefited enormously from a combined approach.

Samples of Project Activity and Reflection Grids

PROJECT ACTIVITY : PLANNING GRID					
ACTIVITY	INTENDED OUTCOME / TARGETS	WHO INVOLVED -LANG(S) -TEACHERS - PUPILS (CLASS & ABILITY)	TIME SCALE / DEADLINES	METHODS USED	MONITORING PROCEDURES
* Exploit oral aspect of unit in pair work * Make sure pupils change partner often during pair work practice * Use of worksheets to help giving and compiling information about oneself and one's partner	Pupils learn and become confident in asking and giving extended information about themselves and others	LANGUAGE: GERMAN TEACHER: ULLA PEARSON CLASS 9 OE/SET 1 MOTHER TONGUE ENGLISH – GOOD WELSH LEARNERS	4-5 weeks	TEACHER PRESENTATIONS TO WHOLE CLASS (FLASH CARDS CASSETTE COURSE BOOK) Pupil centred activities - pair work - group work - role-plays - worksheets	Video recordings of class activities

* combine learnt materials from unit 1+2

PROJECT ACTIVITY : REFLECTION GRID						
WHAT HAPPENED	SUCCESSES	FAILURES	REFLECTIONS : PUPILS / TEACHERS / OBSERVER(S)	EVIDENCE (e.g. lesson plans, notes, materials, video/audio)	OTHER COMMENTS (← problems)	ACTION TO BE TAKEN
① A week-end job activity for this interview went very well	→ oral success. Work to do with this topic was entered for the Eisteddfod and two pupils won 1. and 2 prize		PUPILS: TEACHERS: OBSERVER(S):	-recording of interview - video of class activities	① Teaching in non-specialists' classroom difficult as no visual support material can be put on wall	① Make use of flash cards of pupil-teacher interaction phrases and put on board in each lesson
② Going shopping for clothes	→	Had to be cut short as too much time had been spent on activity (1)			② group work difficult in formal classroom setting	→ rearrange tables at beginning of lesson
③ Pupil assessment		③ Pupils' self monitoring sheet did not work. They did not take it seriously			③ artificial situation of speaking German when coming straight from other lessons	→ warm-up dialog in every lesson "Hallo, wie geht's? Was hast du gestern abend gemacht?"
					④ Total target language approach seems to slow down classroom work	

PROJECT ACTIVITY : REFLECTION GRID						
WHAT HAPPENED	SUCCESSES	FAILURES	REFLECTIONS : PUPILS / TEACHERS / OBSERVER(S)	EVIDENCE (e.g. lesson plans, notes, materials, video/audio)	OTHER COMMENTS	ACTION TO BE TAKEN
The more complex the language becomes the more difficult it is to maintain momentum and keep the pupils speaking in foreign tongues.	Chapter 6 in RN 1 is highly motivating as it deals with food everybody's favourite, so this last half-term has been a good one as far as oral work is concerned	Even though the pupils still enjoy the CALL, they are not so keen to use the personal recorders, mainly because they think that they're going to sound silly and they are afraid of mispronouncing words.	PUPILS: Welsh-medium 7Y are not so keen in using the cassette-recorders. TEACHERS: English-medium 7N are now in trainee teacher's supervision. OBSERVER(S):	as per last sheet.	Year 7 will soon have to face an assessment as their main report for the year is due next half-term. So I will have to focus a lot more on other skills in class for a while	

Schools involved in the Project were required to complete Planning and Reflection Grids every half-term; see examples on previous page. On the Planning Grid, teachers were invited to write in what activity was proposed and its intended outcome or targets. The teacher and class were noted along with a timescale, methods to be used and monitoring procedures. After the event, a Reflection Grid was filled in describing what happened, successes and failures, and any comments from pupils, teacher or other observer. Notes were entered giving the lesson evidence (plans, materials, etc.), follow-up comments and resultant action to be taken. These grids were designed in consultation with the schools themselves and proved that there are no hard and fast rules about what works and what doesn't. Copies of the grids were sent to the relevant Field Officer. As *Darland* found, using the grids made it easier to link activities to on-going classroom topics. Although more able pupils participated more willingly in a number of the activities mentioned in the Teaching section, schools reported that because of departmental collaboration, differentiation was not difficult to achieve. The feeling was that pupils with special educational needs coped well. Teachers averred that the very fact of having to complete and submit the grids concentrated the mind, clarified ideas and provided immediate and effective evaluation.

It may be useful to departments to have a few ideas for workshops sessions to kick-start the brainstorming process. The following activities represent the crux of the work carried out by the project schools and offer a base from which each department will identify its own priorites and routes.

Departmental priorities checklist

- Develop activities to reduce or eliminate written language support.
- Develop ways and means of motivating pupils to speak more and to want to speak more.
- Develop activities designed to increase learner confidence.
- Develop strategies for simple, regular, non-threatening assessment of speaking skills.
- Develop activities to improve pronunciation, intonation and fluency.
- Develop activities to provide pupils with creative and imaginative speaking opportunities.
- Develop pupils' independence and initiative.
- Develop the use of songs, raps and games for enjoyment and motivation and to encourage initiative.
- Develop open-ended drama techniques, giving pupils a measure of control.

Having planned the activities and prepared appropriate materials, departments should then establish what else they need and make sure that they have all the other supporting materials necessary. Mention has already been made of wall posters, ceiling mobiles and so on. Specific materials for games may be needed: cards, dice, 'jetons', playing boards, stopwatches, blu-tack, tape-recorders. IT hardware and software may need to be in place. OHPs, OHT acetates, marker pens and the like should be at hand if required. This, of course, has implications for the setting-up of lessons. If all materials are ready to use without losing time in lessons, then any given activity will have maximum impact.

Whatever the activities used to develop pupils' speaking skills, teachers found that they had, at some stage, to turn their attention to the learning environment and classroom organisation. Different activities made different demands and required different support mechanisms. The need to display supportive language posters became self-evident. One department decided to put themselves in the pupils' place in order to determine and prioritise what pupils needed. However this is approached, the HMI Survey acknowledged: '*In the best practice, there are departmental guidelines and an agreed common format for the support materials exhibited.*' The physical layout of the classroom and the grouping of pupils deserve consideration so that they fit the activity and encourage the desired objectives. 'Fitness for Purpose' is an oft-used maxim but it can be a useful reminder, for organisation as much as for planning.

With resources in place, teachers were beginning to move on to consider how they could further develop their use. Even with the wonderful resource of the *Eurovillage*, the teachers in Gwendraeth were soon discussing how to develop the use of its realistic setting beyond the immediately obvious. This resulted in increasingly imaginative scenarios, particularly at KS4. Other schools similarly deliberated on ways to extend the boundaries of pupils' speaking by extending the use of the resources available, from role-play cards to comic strips, from the video camera to the school building itself.

Modern Language departments undertaking a speaking skills project need the support of the school and its management. As has been seen, the requisite resources and equipment have to be made or obtained. There may well be financial implications and the allocation of capitation and development funding should be sensitive to perceived needs. The amount of curriculum time afforded modern languages, often felt to be inadequate, might be looked at. A school can offer support by way of encouragement and by publicly valuing what the pupils achieve. The *Eurovillage* could not have been built without the help of many people both within that school and interested parties in the community. Schools can provide an audience for pupils to perform to — at *eisteddfodau*, for example. The whole school can participate in events such as 'European Days' or 'Language Festivals'. The consequent rise in the value of the subject in the eyes of the pupils is inestimable. Support may be available from outside agencies, including local businesses, particularly if they have dealings with Europe. It may be possible to visit other schools to learn from their experiences and to compare one's own.

If any modern language teachers have doubts about the desirability of initiating a similar project in their school or their ability to develop it successfully, a comment from the end-of-project report by Pembroke may help: '*Since embarking on the Project, the level of interaction between Staff has increased considerably . . . This sharing has generated a feast of ideas and strategies, and proved that we are more imaginative and inventive than we thought we were!*'

CiLT